FOR

DUMMIES®

PORTABLE EDITION

by Sue Jenkins

WILEY

John Wiley & Sons, Inc.

Tumblr™ For Dummies®, Portable Edition

Published by
John Wiley & Sons, Inc.
111 River Street
Hoboken, NJ 07030-5774
www.wiley.com

WILEY

About the Author

Sue Jenkins is a web and graphic designer, an award-winning software instructor, Adobe Certified Instructor/Adobe Certified Expert, fine art photographer, and founder of Luckychair. com. She is the author of several *For Dummies* instructional books on web design, Dreamweaver, Illustrator, and Photoshop, including *Web Design All-in-One For Dummies* (Wiley) and *Smashing Photoshop CS5: 100 Professional Techniques* (Wiley/ SmashingMagazine). In addition, Sue is the software instructor in seven training programs from ClassOnDemand. com and Lynda. com, a part-time instructor at Noble Desktop in New York City, and an Assistant Professor of graphic design at Marywood University in northeastern PA. For questions, tips, and inspiration, follow her on Facebook, Tumblr, and Twitter.

Dedication

To Kyle, 8, for loving me all the way through, and for being the best son in the whole wide world. (Kyle's words, which express my feelings perfectly.)

Author's Acknowledgments

My first thank you is to all the people at Tumblr for creating such a cool micro-blogging platform that's not only free, but also super fun to use. Big giant thank you's go second to my awesome agent, Matt Wagner, who continues to surprise me with sweet projects like this book, which was such a blast to write. To acquisitions editor, Amy Fandrei, I thank for her help with getting the project off the ground and gently but firmly pushing things along. Praise also goes to my delightful project editor, Kim Darosett, who has an amazing ability to look at the big picture and move all the pieces around until they fit together beautifully. Special thanks also go to Barry Childs-Helton, my copy editor, and James Russell, my technical editor, for their excellent comments and suggestions. Generous thanks also go to my production coordinator, Kristie Rees, for all her hard work, and to all the other folks at Wiley who were a part of this project for their fantastic effort at making this book look great. This is goofy, but I'd also like to thank Bravo and Lifetime for having such bizarre and wildly entertaining reality TV shows like Project Runway and Big Rich Texas that help me unwind after a long day of writing. Lastly, thanks to Kyle and Phil. You make me smile.

Publisher's Acknowledgments

We're proud of this book; please send us your comments at http://dummies. custhelp.com. For other comments, please contact our Customer Care Department within the U.S. at 877-762-2974, outside the U.S. at 317-572-3993, or fax 317-572-4002.

Some of the people who helped bring this book to market include the following:

Acquisitions and Editorial

Project Editor: Kim Darosett

Acquisitions Editor: Amy Fandrei

Senior Copy Editor: Barry Childs-Helton

Technical Editor: James H. Russell

Editorial Manager: Leah Michael

Editorial Assistant: Leslie Saxman

Sr. Editorial Assistant: Cherie Case

Cover Photo: © iStockphoto.com / Cienpies Design

Cartoons: Rich Tennant (www. the5thwave.com)

Composition Services

Project Coordinator: Kristie Rees

Layout and Graphics: Melanee Habig, Sennett Vaughan Johnson, Lavonne Roberts

Proofreaders: Lindsay Amones, Rebecca Denoncour

Indexer: Potomac Indexing, LLC

Publishing and Editorial for Technology Dummies

 Richard Swadley, Vice President and Executive Group Publisher

 Andy Cummings, Vice President and Publisher

 Mary Bednarek, Executive Acquisitions Director

 Mary C. Corder, Editorial Director

Publishing for Consumer Dummies

 Kathleen Nebenhaus, Vice President and Executive Publisher

Composition Services

 Debbie Stailey, Director of Composition Services

Contents at a Glance

Table of Contents

Introduction

*W*elcome to *Tumblr For Dummies,* Portable Edition! This book is your personal guide to using Tumblr. In the following pages, you'll discover everything you need to create a Tumblr account, pick a theme, and start blogging.

Did you know that Tumblr currently hosts more than 46 million free blogs on the Internet? With more than 18 billion (yeah, *billion*) total posts, that's more than 55 million posts or 545 million page views happening on Tumblr each day. Sounds like a hot trend, right? It is.

Billed as a "platform for self-expression," Tumblr is the fastest-growing, free micro-blogging social media service that is addictive and fun to use. No matter where you are in the world, no matter what time of day, you can share anything you want on your Tumblr blog including text, photos, quotes, chats, links, music, and video, all from the convenience of your browser, phone, computer desktop, or e-mail. What's more, with over a thousand themes to choose from, you can customize your own Tumblr page with different graphics, colors, and fonts, and even modify a theme's HTML.

You can also connect Tumblr to your Facebook and Twitter accounts so that anytime you post to Tumblr, your other accounts will be updated automatically too. Talk about convenient.

Another reason for Tumblr's popularity is the fact that you can *like* and *reblog* other Tumblr users' posts. Finding out that someone liked your post or reblogged it is a special feeling that makes you want to post more.

Tumblr users are interested in all kinds of things, making it one of the most fun sites to explore on the Internet. If all this sounds like it might be interesting to you, then read on to learn how to get in on the Tumblr action and become part of this exciting new world.

About This Book

This *Tumblr For Dummies* book is what you might call a reference book. You can read it sequentially from cover to cover, or you can just as easily skip around to find out more about specific topics as your need arises. That way, if you come across a section that you already know about or don't think applies to you, you can skip that part or return to it at another time.

There is no need for you to memorize anything in this book. Instead, you can always refer back to a particular section or use Tumblr's Help Center to find the answer to a specific question you may have.

This book covers the same topics you'd want to know about if you were to explore the site on your own. Each chapter is written in a clear and straightforward manner so you can focus on the learning without having to worry about vocabulary or digesting any complicated technical mumbo jumbo.

Conventions Used in This Book

To help you with understanding some of the technical aspects of using Tumblr, you'll find certain typographic rules and conventions used throughout this book. Specifically, any new terms, web addresses, and code examples will be styled differently from the regular text. Here's an overview:

- **New terms:** Any new terms mentioned in this book are set apart in *italics*.

- **Web addresses:** Several websites are mentioned throughout this book as examples, resources, and references. Each web address is listed in monofont, as in `www.tumblr.com/themes/`.

- **Code examples:** HTML, CSS, JavaScript code examples used in this book are listed in monospaced text, either set apart from the text or within a paragraph, as in the following example:

    If you're familiar with HTML and have access to all the code, you could place this script code before the closing `</head>` tag instead.

Foolish Assumptions

As with all books, a writer must make some assumptions about her readers so that the book can provide a consistent level of information. As such, this book assumes you know some basic technology including how to use a computer and browse the Internet. This book further presumes that you understand how to use a basic text editor to select text and modify its properties.

Beyond that, some basic understanding of *HTML (HyperText Markup Language)* and *CSS (Cascading Style Sheets)* would be great, but it's not necessary. You should know, however, about the following web-related topics:

- ✔ **Web graphics:** It will be helpful for you to know how to create your own web graphics should you want to include any on your Tumblr blog. Creating graphics is quite easy, and there are several free services online that you can use to convert pictures downloaded from your digital camera or cell phone into web-friendly optimized graphics in the *JPG, PNG,* or *GIF* format.

- ✔ **Audio files:** Currently you can only share *MP3* files on Tumblr, so knowing a little about this file format will help you with adding your own sound files into your posts.

- ✔ **Video files:** You can share video files on your Tumblr blog by uploading a video file, inserting the raw Embed-tag from a video/flash site, or by linking to a file on YouTube, Vimeo, or some other video-sharing website.

This book is chock-full of interesting tidbits, so you'll likely discover all kinds of new technology, services, and websites in each chapter. With an open mind and a playful spirit, reading through these pages should be a fun and engaging adventure, especially after you start blogging with Tumblr.

Icons Used in This Book

This book uses a handful of special icons to help make your reading experience a little easier. You'll find the icons in the left margin next to things I think are extra important or that you may find particularly interesting.

Tip icons are used for providing you with special hints, tricks, links, or special notes about a particular topic that you might not discover on your own.

If you see a Warning icon in the text, it means there's something important that warrants your attention. Warnings are designed to help you avoid common mistakes or give your important suggestions about a particular topic.

Technical Stuff icons are placed next to topics that might be a little on the techy side, but that you should still pay attention to. For instance, you may learn about a special feature or workaround that can help you accomplish a specific task.

The Remember icon highlights important information about Tumblr that's worth committing to memory.

Where to Go from Here

Now that you have a general understanding of what topics this book covers, it's time to jump in and start having fun!

Definitely read Chapter 1 to discover how to sign up and set up your blog. You'll also want to check out Chapter 2 to find out about all the different kinds of posts you can make with your Tumblr account. After that, you can either read the rest of the book in order or scan through the Table of Contents or Index to find what interests you.

Occasionally, we have updates to our technology books. If this book does have technical updates, they will be posted at www.dummies.com/go/tumblrupdates.

Chapter 1

Setting Up Your Tumblr Blog

*T*umblr is the fastest-growing free blogging platform on the Internet, and with good reason. It's intuitive and easy to use; one of the first things you'll notice about Tumblr is how quickly you can create an account and start blogging.

In this chapter, you find out how to create a Tumblr account, set your account preferences, and edit them, if needed. You also discover how to select and apply one of several free themes to your Tumblr blog to give it some personality. Lastly, you get a look at the option of customizing your site information so visitors can learn more about you and what your blog is all about.

Creating Your Account

To create your first Tumblr account, follow these steps:

1. **Start by visiting** www.tumblr.com, **where you see the signup screen as shown in Figure 1-1.**

Figure 1-1: The Tumblr signup screen.

2. **In the first two fields, enter a valid e-mail address and a password of your choice.**

3. **In the URL field, enter a name for your blog.**

   The name can be anything you like, such as your name or a title that describes your blog. If another member already has the blog name you want, keep trying new names until you find one that is available. When selecting a name, keep in mind that because hosting and storage are free to users, all new sites are created as subdomains of the Tumblr website. This means that if you name your Tumblr account "spoonobsession," your Tumblr web address becomes spoonobsession.tumblr.com.

   You may change the URL of your Tumblr account at any time on your Blog Settings page. In addition, you may delete unused accounts and create new ones at any time.

4. **After you've filled out all the fields on the signup screen, click the Start Posting! button.**

   If you see the anti-spam CAPTCHA dialog box, enter the text you see onscreen in the text field and click the I'm Human! button to proceed.

5. **Next, check your e-mail.**

   Tumblr sends you a welcome e-mail within the hour to verify your e-mail address. In most cases, you'll only have to wait five to ten minutes.

6. **To finalize the account setup process, click the link inside the verification e-mail from Tumblr.**

   Huzzah! You now have a Tumblr blog!

Selecting Your Account Settings

Looking at your new account in the Dashboard for the first time might seem a tad confusing, but you'll quickly learn how it works. While you could jump right in and follow the on-screen prompts shown in Figure 1-2 to make your first post, pick a theme, or change your avatar, I focus on starting by selecting your account settings.

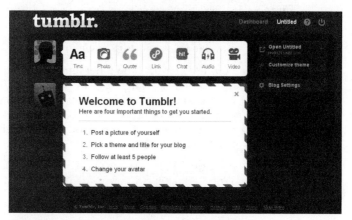

Figure 1-2: Navigating around the Tumblr dashboard.

To access your account settings, follow these steps:

1. Click the Blog Settings button located in the sidebar on the right side of the page.

This brings you to the Settings page, shown in Figure 1-3, where you can customize certain aspects of your blogging experience such as adding a portrait photo and deciding whether to share your Tumblr posts on your Facebook page.

Figure 1-3: The Tumblr Settings page.

2. Customize these settings as desired:

- *Portrait Photo:* To add a personalized portrait photo or identifying avatar graphic, click the Choose File button to browse for and select an image from your computer or networked drive. Once selected, the name of your image file appears to the right of the Choose File button.

   For best results, use a square image that is 128 x 128 pixels or larger, 10 MB (megabytes) max (though smaller file sizes will load faster), in one of the following formats: JPG, GIF, PNG, or BMP.

- *URL:* The URL field should automatically display the name you selected when you signed up, such as http://spoonobsession.tumblr.com. You may also use this field to change the URL of your blog at any time. You also have the option here to set a custom domain name. This is only recommended for users who are familiar with domain registration, hosting, and DNS transfers. For information about setting a custom domain name for your Tumblr blog, visit www.tumblr.com/docs/en/custom_domains.

- *Replies:* Tumblr offers options for allowing replies from people you follow as well as replies from people who have been following you for two or more weeks. Click one or both check boxes to enable these options. To disallow replies of any kind, leave both boxes unchecked.

- *Ask:* If you want visitors to ask questions that you can answer on your blog, check this box, and a link to a new Ask page appears on your blog. You may also customize the Ask page title and enable an option that allows anonymous questions. To help you see how Ask inquiries look when they arrive, Tumblr's Tumblrbot will instantly send a question to your Tumblr Inbox.

Tumblr recommends you use the Anonymous option with caution by displaying a warning message that says anonymous comments can sometimes "get nasty." In other words, if the comments get out of hand, turn this feature off.

- *Submissions:* Check this box to allow people to Submit posts for possible publication on your blog. Once clicked, a link for this option displays on your blog. Submissions are good, for example, if you intend to showcase themed content submitted by others, such as moustaches (see lovestache.tumblr.com, for example). Once selected, you will see additional options to customize the Submissions page title, provide visitors with submission guidelines, and choose which types of posts will be accepted (text, photo, quote, link, or video).

When Ask and/or Submit options are enabled, an envelope icon that displays in the upper-right area of your blog's Dashboard will indicate incoming messages. You may then choose to respond to Ask messages publicly, privately, or ignore them. Likewise, submissions may be published or not, either with or without the sender's information.

- *Facebook:* Check this box if you have a Facebook account and want to share your Tumblr posts on your Facebook page. Selecting this option opens either a Facebook Log In window where you enter your Facebook e-mail and password to log in and link accounts, or a Facebook window asking you to Allow Tumblr access.

- *Twitter:* To link your existing Twitter account to Tumblr, check this box and click the Sign In with Twitter button. When the Twitter authorization window opens, enter your account information and click the Authorize App button to log in and link your accounts.

- *Post by Email:* Tumblr automatically generates a random e-mail address that you can use to create posts by e-mail. To reset this e-mail address for security purposes at any time, click the Reset button.

- *RSS Feeds:* If your blog is public rather than private, the blog will have an RSS feed that can be viewed at any time by adding "/rss" to the end of the blog URL. To make feed viewers visit your blog to read full posts, enable the Truncate RSS feed checkbox. If you use FeedBurner for RSS, you may link the RSS of Tumblr to that account by putting a check in this check box and clicking the FeedBurner link to sign in to your FeedBurner account.

- *Language:* Select your desired language. English is the default setting for U.S. accounts.

- *Timezone:* Choose your time zone.

- *Directory:* This section has two options. The Allow Search Engines to Index Your Blog option is selected by default. Deselect it if you don't want your blog indexed. NSFW stands for Not Safe For Work. If your blog includes explicit content, check this box.

If for any reason you want to delete your account, click the Delete Your Account link at the bottom of the listing.

3. **When you've finished entering or editing your account settings, click the Save button.**

   You may return to this page at any time to edit these settings.

Setting Your Account Preferences

The next place to go to customize how your Tumblr blog functions is Preferences. Follow these steps to set your preferences:

1. **Click the icon at the top of the page that looks like a round spoked gear.**

   The Preferences page appears, as shown in Figure 1-4.

Preferences

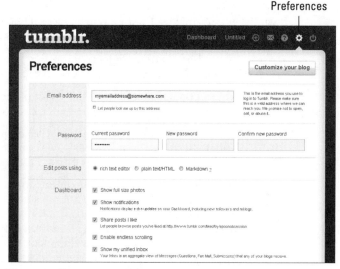

Figure 1-4: The Tumblr Preferences page.

2. **Set the following options as desired:**

   • *Email Address:* The e-mail address you used to create the account will be listed here. To change this e-mail to another address, enter it here. The option to let people look you up by this address is enabled by default. Deselect it to keep this e-mail address private.

   • *Password:* The current password is displayed here as encrypted dots. To change your password, enter your new password in the New Password and Confirm New Password fields.

- *Edit Posts Using:* Tumblr's default option for author-
ing and editing posts is Rich Text Editor, which
allows you to type and format text using a set of
buttons, but does not allow for advanced HTML/
CSS coding. This is the best option to use if you
are unfamiliar with HTML or only need simple text
editing tools such as Bold, Italic, List, and so on. To
code your posts in Plain text/HTML or Markdown
instead, however, select the desired option. To
learn more about Markdown, click the tiny question
mark link to the right of that option.

- *Dashboard:* Choose the options you would like to
have enabled for your Tumblr blog.

  Show Full Size Photos: When enabled, visitors can
  click a photo in a blog post to view it full size.

  Show Notifications: Select this setting to have notifications display updates on your dashboard.

  Share Posts I Like: Choose this to let others browse
  the posts you like on a dedicated "liked by" page.

  Enable Endless Scrolling: This feature allows visitors to scroll content endlessly, without having to
  click a link to view previous posts. Pretty neat.

  Show My Unified Inbox: This option appears only if
  you've enabled the Ask and Submission features in
  your Settings. When enabled, Tumblr will keep all
  your messages, such as questions and submissions,
  in one place and add an envelope icon to your
  Dashboard. When this box is unchecked, messages
  are accessible only through the Messages button
  on the sidebar.

- *Language:* Select your language if other than English.

- *Email Notifications:* Select these options to be noti-
fied by e-mail when you get New Followers, Reblogs
of your posts, and New Messages from visitors.

3. **Right above the Cancel button are two links for additional preference settings:**

- *Block Other Users:* To block a URL or a particular
user from your Tumblr blog, click this link and
enter the URL or username to block.

- *Delete Your Account:* To delete your account, click this link and confirm deletion by entering your account password. Keep in mind; once it's gone, it's gone.

4. **To save the changes you've made on this page, click the Save button. Otherwise, click the Cancel button and you will be returned to the Dashboard.**

You may return to this area at any time to edit these settings.

Customizing Your Blog

Up to this point, you may have noticed that your blog has the name *Untitled* displaying at the top of the page and uses the default Redux theme with the plain blue background, which probably doesn't reflect your personality very well. Fortunately, you can fix that by customizing your blog.

All the appearance settings for your blog are located on the Customize page. To access the Customize page, shown in Figure 1-5, click the word Untitled at the top of your screen, then click the option called Customize Theme in the right sidebar.

Theme customization options

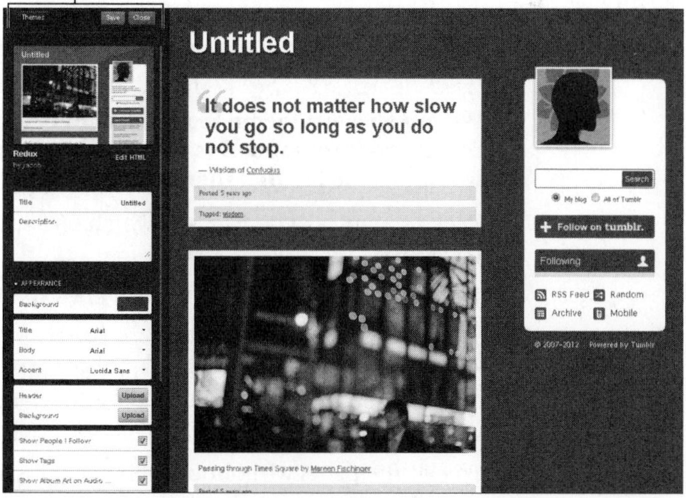

Figure 1-5: Use the Tumblr Customize page to modify your blog's appearance.

You can also access this page by clicking the Customize Your Blog button at the top right of the Preferences page (refer to Figure 1-4).

In this section, you find out how to use the Customize page to select a theme, set a blog title and description, and make other appearance and layout changes to show off your personal style.

Selecting a theme

By default, all new accounts use the blue Redux theme, but you can easily preview, select, and apply new themes at any time. Follow these steps to select an alternate theme:

1. **On the Customize page, click the Themes button to view a listing of themes.**

   This button is located at the top of the left pane.

2. **Scroll up and down through the list of paid and free themes.**

   Use the drop-down menu to narrow your theme search to a category such as Free Themes, Two Column, or Minimalistic.

   If desired, you can search through even more themes in Tumblr's theme garden at www.tumblr.com/themes/. For additional details about theme customization, installing new themes, and modifying existing themes, check out Chapter 9.

3. **When you see a theme that looks interesting, click that theme's thumbnail to preview how your blog would look using that theme.**

   Click as many as you like; see which one appeals to you most.

4. **To begin using a selected theme, click the Use button at the top of the left panel.**

   If you chose a paid theme, click the Use button, then click the Purchase button, and follow the onscreen prompts to enter your name and credit card information.

   To exit the panel without changing themes, click the Cancel button.

Setting the title and description

The title and description appear at the top of your blog. In the left pane, you can customize both fields to let visitors learn more about you and your blog:

- ✔ **Title:** The title is the name or phrase that appears at the top of your blog. This can be the same as your blog name, something completely different, or you could even leave it blank. To edit the title, simply double-click the word Untitled (and type in your new title text).

- ✔ **Description:** The description helps define what your blog is all about, whether it's a short bio or a brief statement about your blog's purpose. To add a description, click inside the Description field and start typing. Your text will appear instantly within the theme so you can easily proofread and edit as needed.

If you know HTML, you can include any HTML code in the Title and Description fields. For example, if you want to include a link in the Description area to your Twitter account, you could enter the following HTML, making sure to replace your Twitter account name where it says *NAME*:

```
<a href=https://twitter.com/#!/NAME>Twitter
</a>
```

The style and formatting for the Title and Description fields, as well as where those attributes are located within the blog theme, are controlled by the theme's CSS (Cascading Style Sheets). If you know how to edit CSS, click the Edit HTML button that appears above the title.

Customizing the Appearance

Some themes allow you to customize their appearance. Any theme-specific options appear at the top of the Appearance section of the Customize Theme panel. For example, you may have the option to change theme colors, fonts, and font sizes, upload header and background images, and input your Google Analytics ID.

Look through the Appearance section for your theme to determine which features you can customize. To change a theme option, click the field and follow the onscreen prompts:

- ✔ **Colors:** If a color box appears next to a setting listed in the Appearance area, you can click the color box to adjust the color. When you're finished selecting a new color from the pop-up color picker, click the X to close the color picker.

- ✔ **Fonts:** Most themes have a default font selected. If a font menu is presented, scroll through the list and choose a font that appeals to you.

- ✔ **Uploads:** Some themes let you upload your own background or header images. If no recommended sizes are specified, upload your desired image to see how it fits into the theme. Then, if necessary, use a photo-editing program such as Adobe Photoshop to resize the image so it fits better in the theme.

- ✔ **Optional features:** Some theme features can be toggled on and off by selecting or deselecting a check box. For example, you may have the option of showing the date on the index page or enabling infinite scrolling.

- ✔ **Social media ID:** If your theme includes fields for social media, such as Twitter, Flickr, and Google Analytics, you can enter your account credentials to link those accounts to your Tumblr blog.

In addition to theme-specific options, the Appearance area also includes fields for linking your Tumblr with other social media accounts such as Google Analytics, Disqus (a comments platform at http://disqus.com/ that integrates nicely with Tumblr), Pinterest, and Facebook. To add icons or links to those accounts enter the appropriate information as indicated in each field.

In addition to all these customizable options, you should see a Reset Defaults link at the bottom of the Appearance area. If you want to return your selected theme to the way it was when you first installed it, click the Reset Defaults link.

Creating pages

Like other blogging platforms, Tumblr gives you the option of creating additional pages for your blog, such as an About or Contact page. To add a new page, follow these steps:

1. **Expand the Pages category on the left panel.**

2. **Click the + Add a Page link to open the Add Page window, shown in Figure 1-6.**

Figure 1-6: Use the Add Page dialog box to build new pages for your Tumblr blog.

3. **Choose the desired layout type based on your knowledge of HTML/CSS. Here are your choices:**

   • *Standard Layout:* Select the Standard Layout option from the drop-down menu to add a new page with the default theme layout.

   • *Custom Layout:* Select the Custom Layout option to enter the URL and HTML/CSS for a new page using your custom layout. With this option, enter your URL at the top and your custom HTML/CSS in the blank field below, and then click the Create Page button.

   • *Redirect:* To make a *redirect page,* where the visitor clicks a link and goes to another page (either within or outside your website), enter the page URL and the desired redirect link.

4. **For Standard Layouts, enter the page URL and title, and click the Show a Link to This Page check box if you want this page to be accessible from all the other pages on your blog.**

5. **In the Body area, enter your page content.**

   This can include text, lists, images, and links. You may also add custom HTML/CSS by clicking the HTML button.

6. **When finished, click the Create Page button. Otherwise, click Cancel to close the window without adding a new page.**

   Links to any new pages you create here will appear at the top of your blog.

Selecting Advanced options

The last part of the Customize page is setting Advanced options that control how your Tumblr account is displayed in a browser or on a handheld or mobile device. To change these settings, follow these steps:

1. **Expand the Advanced category on the left panel, as shown in Figure 1-7.**

Figure 1-7: Set Advanced options in the Advanced section of the Customize Theme page.

2. **Set the following options as desired:**

- *Number of Posts Per Page:* The default is set to 10 but you can change it to any number between 1 and 15. If your theme allows for an option called Infinite Scroll and you have enabled it, leave the number set at 10.

- *Open Links in New Window:* Check here to make links on your Tumblr site to open a new browser tab or window. Leave it unchecked to have links to open within the same window.

- *Use Optimized Mobile Layout:* Leave this option checked to ensure that your theme is mobile-device-friendly. Keep in mind, however, that it may override (read: break) some parts of your theme's design to improve browsing on mobile devices.

- *Use Descriptive URLs:* This is a smart option that embeds your keyword tags within your URLs to help make your pages more search-engine-friendly. For instance, Tumblr may change the URL for your post from just numbers to something with a text summary such as `yoursite.tumblr.com/post/12345/eating-cake`. Only private blogs may want to disable this feature.

- *Promote Tumblr!:* Keep this option checked to have a Follow button added to your blog so that non-Tumblr visitors can join Tumblr and start following you.

- *Add Custom CSS:* To add any custom CSS to style and position content on your site, enter it here. You may also add CSS to the theme's code by clicking the Edit HTML button at the top of the Customize page. For example, if you want to override the current color for all <p> tags and make it orange, you'd enter:

  ```
  p {color: #FF9900;}
  ```

To modify the theme's code directly, click the Edit HTML button at the top of the Customize Theme page. You can get the lowdown on this feature in the section about editing a theme's HTML in Chapter 9.

3. **When you've finished entering your Advanced settings, click the green Save button at the top of the page.**

4. **To close the Customize page and return to your Dashboard, click the Close button.**

To see how your new theme and customized settings look, click your newly titled Tumblr blog link at the top of the screen next to where it says Dashboard (or if you've created more than one blog with the same e-mail address, select your blog by name from the My Blogs menu icon); then click the Open link at the top of the sidebar. The link opens your page in a new browser tab or window.

Chapter 2

Creating Your First Post

● ●

● ●

*T*here are seven kinds of posts that you can create with Tumblr: text, photo, quote, link, chat, audio, and video. Each post type has its own distinct form that you fill in to create a new post. Alongside each form, you see a list of general posting options. These options are the same regardless of post type, and you can fill them in on the fly each time you create new post. In addition, many of the new post forms share a common formatting toolbar.

In this chapter, you find about all the general posting and formatting options, followed by step-by-step instructions for creating each post type.

Exploring the General Posting and Formatting Options

For every new post on Tumblr, you have the opportunity to specify some general options to enhance your posts. In addition, for posts that include text, you see the same row of formatting buttons. Here is a brief overview of these general posting and formatting options.

Using the sidebar posting options

When you click one of the seven "new post" icons at the top of your Dashboard, the sidebar posting options appear on the right side of the page, as shown in Figure 2-1.

Formatting buttons   Posting options

Figure 2-1: General posting options appear on the right side of the page; text-formatting buttons appear on a bar within the new post form.

Here's a summary of the options:

✔ **Publish menu:** Use this menu to choose when your new post will appear on your Tumblr blog. The default option is *Publish Now,* but you may also select *Add to Queue* or *Publish On* to publish at a specific date and time, *Save as Draft* to publish at a later date, or *Private* to publish a post that only you (and any specified blog administrators) can see.

✔ **Post Date:** You may specify a date for your post, whether that's today, sometime in the future, or sometime in the past. If you leave this field blank, today's date (now) will be applied to your post.

- ✔ **Content Source:** If relevant, enter the URL of the website where the content you're posting was first published.

- ✔ **Tags:** *Tags* are keywords or phrases, such as `photography` or `black and white`, that you use to help visitors and search engines find posts about a specific topic. Enter each tag, one at a time, separated by commas or by pressing the Enter/Return key. If you make a mistake or typo, you can delete any tag by clicking the X next to it.

- ✔ **Set a Custom Post URL:** To add keywords to your post's URL, enter the words here. For example, if you create a post about cupcakes, you can set the custom post URL to `/cupcakes`.

- ✔ **Let People Photo Reply:** If you'd like to ask visitors a question on a text post or caption, end your post with a question mark (?), and the option to let people answer will appear on your blog text, photo, link, audio, or video post. To allow visitors to post photos in their replies, check this box.

- ✔ **Highlight This Post:** Select this option to call attention to your post with a simple rectangular sidebar pointer for $1. The sidebar pointer displays outside the post area, usually on the right side of the page, and points to that particular post. Once you enable this option, you may choose the text that displays on the pointer from a menu, add an icon, and customize the pointer color.

  You may add this new feature only before clicking the Create Post button.

Of course, all these general post settings are optional. If you don't want to fill any of them in, simply leave them blank.

Understanding the text formatting options

In addition to the sidebar options, all posts, with the exception of Link and Chat, include universal text formatting buttons. Use the following buttons to format your content, as shown from left to right in Figure 2-1:

- **Bold/Italic/Strikethrough:** Click any of these toggle buttons to apply or remove these formatting options to your selected text.

- **Unordered List/Ordered List:** Click either button to convert selected text into bullets or numbered list items.

- **Blockquote:** This option will indent selected text using the HTML `blockquote` tag.

- **Insert/Edit Image:** To insert an image or edit a previously inserted image, click this button. When the Insert/Edit image dialog box opens, type in the image URL, description, dimensions, and alignment preferences, and then click the Insert button.

- **Insert/Edit Link:** Use this button to convert any selected text or object into a hyperlink. A dialog box will open for you to enter the Link URL, title, and target. When you're finished, click the Insert button to add the new link.

- **Unlink:** Click this button to remove a hyperlink from selected text.

- **Check Spelling:** To run the spell check automatically on your post text, click this button. Spelling errors will be underlined in red. You may right-click an underlined word to choose a correct spelling or alternate suggestion from the context menu. If your post language is other than English, click this button's drop-down link to change the dictionary language to one of 10 another languages.

- **Insert "Read More" Break:** This option is only available for Text posts using the Rich Text Editor. (If you selected the Plain Text/HTML or Markdown post editing method in your Preferences, you won't see this option.) Place your cursor in your text where you'd like the break to occur before clicking this button. When you've saved the post, the content before the break will appear in the post, stopping at the Read More link (which visitors may click to read the full post on a separate page).

- **Edit HTML Source:** If you're familiar with HTML and want to modify the source code, click this button to view a pop-up editor that accepts HTML code. When you're finished editing, click the Update button.

Creating Different Types of Posts

Posting to Tumblr is a very intuitive process, because each post type uses a similar input form and offers you the same general posting and formatting options. In this section, you'll find basic rules for creating a post, followed by in-depth details about each post type. To create a post, follow these general steps:

1. **On the Dashboard, click the button for the type of post you want to create, as shown in Figure 2-2.**

Figure 2-2: To create a new Tumblr post, click one of the seven post types at the top of the Dashboard.

2. **Fill in the information you want to include in your post.**

   The options you see depend on the type of post you're creating. See the following sections for specific options.

3. **Add the basic posting options in the right sidebar as desired.**

   For the lowdown on these options, see the preceding section.

4. **To preview your new post before publishing, click the Preview button.**

5. **Click the Create post button to create the new post.**

   Or click Cancel to cancel the post and return to the Dashboard.

Text

A text post is the most basic type of post in that it has only two fields for you to fill in (refer to Figure 2-1):

✔ **Title (optional):** Enter a title for your post. If no title is needed, leave this field blank.

✔ **Post:** Enter the text for your post in the space provided and use the general formatting buttons as needed.

Photos

Posting photos is a great way to share pictures of your interests with others. In fact, posting photos is so popular that many professional photographers use Tumblr exclusively as a photo blog. You can upload any type of image — including photographs, illustrations, drawings, diagrams, and other graphics.

The file format must be JPG, GIF, PNG, or BMP, and the file size cannot exceed 10 MB.

To create a photo post, fill in the following information on the Upload a Photo page, shown in Figure 2-3:

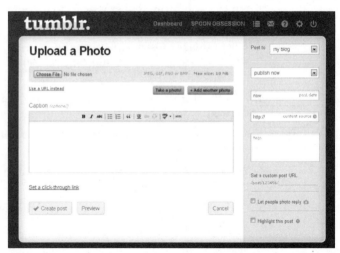

Figure 2-3: Photo posts can have one or more picture, with or without a caption.

✔ **Add a photo:** You can add an image to your post several different ways. Use any of the following methods:

- *Choose File:* Click this button to browse for and select an image on your computer. Once selected, the filename will appear next to the button.

- *Use a URL Instead:* Click this link to specify the location of an image hosted on another website.

- *Take a Photo!:* To use your computer's built-in or peripheral webcam to take a photo, click this button and follow the onscreen prompts to snap the picture.

- *Add Another Photo:* To create photo posts with photosets of two or more pictures, like the example shown in Figure 2-4, click this button as many times as desired, choose your image files, select a layout for the images, and if needed, adjust their placement order. Tumblr will resize all the images and display them in the selected layout.

Fork, Knife, Spoon, Fork, Knife, Spoon, Coffee

#fork #knife #spoon #coffee #photography

Figure 2-4: Create great-looking photo sets with the + Add Another Photo option.

✔ **Caption (optional):** If you want your photo to have a caption or display with additional text, enter it the large text box under Caption. For photosets, you may enter individual captions next to each image.

✔ **Set a Click-Through Link (optional):** Enter the URL of the website this image was sourced from or the URL of the site you'd like visitors to go to after clicking your image.

Quotes

No matter what topics you're interested in, there's bound to be a remarkable quote by somebody about it. For times when you simply must share a quote, click the Quote button on your Tumblr Dashboard.

The Add a Quote form has two sections, one for adding the quote and another for citing the source:

- ✔ **Quote:** Enter your quote in the area provided. No need to worry about quote marks or formatting; the theme should handle that for you, as shown in Figure 2-5.

- ✔ **Source (optional):** Enter the name or other details of the source of your quote in the space provided, and use the general formatting buttons as needed.

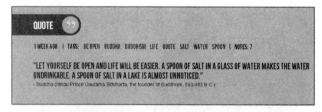

Figure 2-5: Formatting for quote posts is included in your theme.

Links

If you want to make a link to another website the highlight of your Tumblr post, click the Link button on your Tumblr Dashboard. The Link form, shown in Figure 2-6, includes three sections:

- ✔ **Title (optional):** Enter a title for your link. Titles are useful when links include funky characters and numbers (rather than descriptive keywords) in the path name.

✔ **URL:** Enter the URL of the link you want to share.

Be sure to include the `http://` or other protocol before the `www` in the web address.

✔ **Add a Description (optional):** Click the Add a Description text link below the URL field to expand the Description field (see Figure 2-6) where you may enter descriptive text about your link.

Figure 2-6: Create a link post when you'd like to share a link to another site. Title and description are optional.

Chats

Chat posts are perfect for times when you want to share a dialogue with your Tumblr followers. For example, you may have had a funny conversation with a co-worker recently, read something poignant in a book, or overheard an exchange about a current event. Figure 2-7 shows an example of how you might use the chat form.

Figure 2-7: Use the Chat form to share a conversation with your Tumblr followers.

No need to worry about formatting for chats; how it looks when published is coded into your Tumblr theme. All you need to do is enter a title and the dialogue:

- ✔ **Title (optional):** Enter a title for your chat if you think it needs one.

- ✔ **Dialogue:** Enter the conversation, making sure to label each speaker in the dialogue with a name followed by a colon, as in

  Tourist: Could you tell me how to get to Carnegie Hall?

  New Yorker: Yes. Practice!

Audio files

If you are into creating podcasts or posting your favorite music or audio recordings, you'll love adding sound files to your blog with this feature.

To post an MP3 audio file on your Tumblr blog (sorry, no other audio file types are allowed), either with or without an optional description, fill in the following options on the Add an Audio Post page, shown in Figure 2-8:

Figure 2-8: Share your favorite MP3 audio files on your Tumblr blog.

✔ **Upload:** On the Upload tab, click the Choose File button to browse for and select the desired audio file from your computer.

   Using this feature, you may only upload one MP3 audio file (10MB maximum size) per day.

✔ **Search:** To search for and select an existing audio file from SoundCloud.com's extensive shared sound library, click the Search tab and then enter your search term and choose from the list of results. After you've made your selection, the URL to that sound file appears in the External Source URL field.

✔ **External Source:** If you already know the source of an existing MP3 file or SoundCloud URL, click the External Source tab and enter the URL. Sound files are streamed from the URL location and are not hosted by Tumblr.

After selecting your sound file, you can enter an optional description in the Description field, as well as add any of the basic posting options from the sidebar.

Some, but not all, music tracks on SoundCloud include the artist name, track name, album name, and album art. You can add to or edit this track information at any time after posting the audio file by clicking the post's Edit link in the Dashboard.

Videos

Everyone loves a good video; on Tumblr, you can share your favorite videos directly from sites like YouTube and Vimeo, as well as upload your own video files.

To add a video to your Tumblr blog, click the Video button on the Dashboard and complete the video form shown in Figure 2-9:

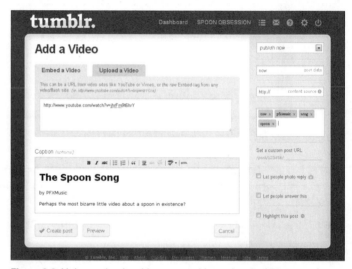

Figure 2-9: Link or upload a video to your blog using the Video post form.

✔ **Embed a Video:** Use the Embed a Video field to enter the URL of a particular video or paste in the raw Embed-tag code from any video/Flash site.

✔ **Upload a Video:** Click the Choose File button to browse for and select a video file from your computer. Before you may create your post, you must provide Tumblr with permission to use the video file under their Terms of Service.

Tumblr allows you to upload up to 5 minutes of video each day, with a 100MB maximum size per file. The site also recommends files that use SWF files or MP4 video and AAC audio that are 500 x 700 pixels or smaller.

After you've selected a video file, you may enter an optional Caption for the video in the large text box under Caption.

Chapter 3

Deciding What Content to Post

· ·

· ·

Knowing *how* to post is only one part of the equation on Tumblr. The other part, knowing *what* to post, takes a little more creative brainpower and is much more fun. In this chapter, I talk about the different ways to use Tumblr to present and share information — and compare blogs that create content with blogs that collect content.

Exploring Topics to Post

While some people and companies use Tumblr strictly as a platform to promote their businesses, most folks use Tumblr as a personal blogging platform. That is, they use it to share original, personal information that directly relates to what's going on in their life, including text posts, photos, links, video, music, chats, and quotes that support their identity.

As you delve into the world of Tumblr, you might ask yourself which direction you'd like to take your blog: business or personal. If you choose to promote your business, you can create as many static pages as needed to provide general information about your company and services, and use the main Dashboard area to blog regularly on a topic related to your business. This approach can help greatly to generate traffic and attract new customers.

If, on the other hand, you decide to use Tumblr as a tool for personal expression, *what* you choose to share can be directly related to your own unique interests. Here are several ideas based on specific interests:

- ✓ **Photographer/artist:** If you're a photographer or artist, you might be interested in exclusively sharing examples of your work, making your Tumblr into the place you keep your own personal portfolio website, complete with an image gallery and static pages for a bio, resume or curriculum vitae, exhibition list, and contact information.

- ✓ **Graphic/web/interior designer:** Graphic, web, and interior designers might use Tumblr as a place to showcase their abilities and attract new customers. As a designer, you could easily include a gallery of your designs along with customer testimonials and information about how to contact you for new projects.

- ✓ **Jeweler/craftsperson:** With the popularity of hand crafted jewelry, crafts, and furniture (and websites where you can sell your products, like Etsy), having a non-shopping-cart place to virtually display your work puts the emphasis on your craft and skills as an artisan, not on anyone's pocketbook.

- ✓ **Musician/bands:** Musicians can greatly benefit from Tumblr's fast and effective ways to share information with fans. You can post MP3 audio files and videos of new tracks along with other relevant information such as reviews of recent performances, show dates, and photographs of band members.

- ✓ **World traveler:** If you've been bitten by the travel bug, Tumblr is an excellent platform for sharing your adventures from around the world. Post photos, travel logs, diary entries, conversations, video clips, and audio bites to highlight where you've been, who you've met, and what you've seen.

- ✓ **Sports enthusiast:** Sports lovers can use Tumblr to draw attention to their own skills and accomplishments, the skills of a team they belong to, or even a team that they follow closely.

- ✔ **Writer/poet:** Looking for a venue to share your poetry? Writers and poets can use Tumblr as a place to share their talents as writers. Publish poems, short stories, and chapters to larger projects, or simply expound on ideas that aggravate or inspire you.

- ✔ **Film buff:** If you love film/television and want to weigh in with your thoughts and analysis on that topic, use Tumblr as a platform to share things like movie reviews, links to movie trailers, and photos of your favorite actors.

- ✔ **Cook/baker/chef:** If you love to cook, you can use Tumblr as a place to share your favorite recipes, along with step-by-step instructions and photographs showing how to make your favorite foods. Food blogs (especially those with photographs of delicious looking food!) are extremely popular on Tumblr, often attracting many followers.

To get feedback from followers and engage in an ongoing forum-style dialogue, no matter what type of Tumblr blog you create, consider using a free commenting platform powered by Disqus. With Disqus, Tumblr users can converse publicly with followers. This is quite different from Tumblr's Ask feature, which can be public or private and only allows for a single Q and A. For more information about how to configure your Tumblr blog with Disqus, visit www.disqus.com.

Creating versus Collecting Content

Once you've decided *what* to post on your Tumblr blog, the next thing to consider is whether you'll be creating new content, collecting content from other sources, or combining new and collected information on your blog in some kind of interesting and unified way. Of course, there are as many ways to build a blog as there are people, so what you ultimately choose to do is entirely up to you and your imagination.

Creating content

Tumblr blogs that *create* content almost exclusively present original ideas and media related to a single topic or things that reflect an individual or group's personality, interests, or goals. In most cases, this means posting only new and original entries that haven't been taken from anyone or anywhere else, either on the Web or from another source.

The major benefit of this type of blog is that you can almost absolutely bypass any potential legal issues related to copyright infringement. By showing your own work and ideas, you run virtually no risk of being sued, or of having to pay fees or fines for using someone else's work without permission. For instance, you might create a Tumblr blog to illustrate pictures of your daily outfits, the way Jessica Quirk does at `http://whatiwore.tumblr.com` (shown in Figure 3-1).

Figure 3-1: Tumblr blogs with original content put a spotlight on your creative talents.

In addition to being unique, original posts speak to your creativity and your editorial ability to amass new and interesting information related to your general topic.

Collecting content

In contrast to sites that create their own content, Tumblr blogs that *collect* content tend to feature text, photos, videos, music, and other ideas related to a single theme from a wide variety of sources. For example, your blog can be a place to share information on a topic that inspires and motivates you, such as gaming, politics, or interior decorating. Take the Mi Casa Es Su Casa site (`http://micasaessucasa.tumblr.com/`), shown in Figure 3-2. Here the author has curated some incredible photographs of creatively decorated homes — and it's all photos, no text, which keeps the site visually focused on the aesthetically pleasing aspects of interior design.

Figure 3-2: Collect and display content related to a topic you're passionate about.

Collection blogs can focus on virtually any topic no matter how seemingly ordinary or obscure. They can be about something as creative as a place to show examples of interesting card and stationery design (see `http://stationerylove.tumblr.com`) to something as bizarrely hilarious as a site dedicated to photographs of cats with cash (see `www.cashcats.biz`, a Tumblr site that uses a custom domain name), as shown in Figure 3-3.

Some current popular categories for this type of Tumblr site include History, Architecture, Landscape, Cars, Photography, Illustration, Education, Sports, Advertising, Animals, Food, and Humor.

Figure 3-3: Don't be afraid to use a little humor when selecting a topic for your Tumblr blog.

For additional ideas about collecting and creating content, see Chapter 8.

One important thing to keep in mind when collecting content from others is copyright. Because presumably you don't want to make anyone mad or get sued, it's a good idea to include some kind of disclaimer on your blog about material usage. For example, on charmingly addictive The Baby Animal Blog website at http://thebabyanimalblog.tumblr.com, shown in Figure 3-4, the author has posted a disclaimer that reads, "I take no credit for any of these pictures."

There are many different ways you can word this basic idea, of course, but here's a general suggestion of what you might want to say on your site:

> DISCLAIMER:
> All the [pictures/videos/songs—you fill in the blank] featured on this website belong to their respective owners. If you see your [pictures/videos/songs—you fill in the blank] featured and do not want it here, please email us with link and we will remove it right away.

Figure 3-4: Add a disclaimer on your site about using materials from the web.

Chapter 4

Using the Dashboard

· ·

In This Chapter

▶ Getting to know the Dashboard menu

▶ Creating new blogs

▶ Searching for Help

▶ Editing preferences

▶ Logging in and out

▶ Exploring the sidebar

▶ Launching your site

· ·

*W*ith its plain blue background, simple buttons, and icon navigation, your Tumblr account has a lot of parts that look pretty similar from page to page. Thankfully, you can use the Dashboard icons at the top of the screen to get to most of the places that you need to go. After you create your initial Tumblr account, you use your Dashboard to create new blogs, search for help, edit your account preferences, launch your site, and log in to and out of your account from multiple computers and devices.

The other area you'll use quite often to navigate through your Tumblr site is the Dashboard Sidebar, located conveniently on the right side of the page. The buttons on the Sidebar are context specific to support the various options you select on the Dashboard. Read on to find out more about the features on the Tumblr Dashboard and Sidebar.

Using the Dashboard Menu

Tumblr's Dashboard menu is located at the top of your screen and contains several icon links to assist you with navigating through your account. You can tell you're in the right place if the URL (after logging in) in your browser's address bar says www.tumblr.com/dashboard (see Figure 4-1).

Messages Preferences

Add Blog   Help   Log Out

Figure 4-1: The Dashboard Menu helps you navigate through your account.

> **TIP**
>
> If you're logged into your Tumblr blog and can see a little gray button labeled "Dashboard" anywhere on your screen (usually in the top- or bottom-right corner), click that button to get to your account's Dashboard.

The Dashboard stays at the top of the screen on most pages of your account when you're logged in — except when you're customizing your blog's appearance and when you're using the Mass Post Editor (which you find out about in Chapter 6). You can click these buttons at any time to access the following features, which are described in detail in the remaining sections of this chapter: Dashboard, [*Name of your blog*], Add Blog, Inbox (this icon appears only when the Ask and Submit features with a unified Inbox are enabled in your Settings and Preferences), Help, Preferences, and Log Out.

Creating New Blogs

Should you ever decide that you'd like to create new Tumblr blogs in addition to your *primary* blog, you have two options: You can create a new separate primary blog or a new linked additional blog. A separate primary blog is useful if you want to use a different e-mail address or make the new blog totally unrelated to your original blog. In contrast, a new linked blog uses the same e-mail account and password as your original account but with a new URL. The beauty of this type of account is that you can administer all your linked blog accounts from the main Tumblr Dashboard. Not only that, but secondary accounts may even have multiple authors (contributors). Cool!

New primary blog

To make a new blog that is 100% separate from your existing blog account, log out of your current blog, return to Tumblr's main create account page, and create a new account with a different e-mail address, password, and URL (as described in Chapter 1). Then, each time you want to manage a particular blog, you will need to log in with the appropriate e-mail address, password, and URL, make your changes, and log out.

New additional blog

To create a new additional blog that is linked to your primary account, follow these steps:

1. **Click the Add Blog (+) icon on the Tumblr Dashboard.**

   This opens the Create a New Blog page, shown in Figure 4-2.

Figure 4-2: Add a new secondary linked blog to your primary account on the Create a New Blog page.

2. **In the Title field, enter the title for your new blog.**

   You can change the title at any time after you create the blog by clicking the Customize Theme button on the Dashboard Sidebar.

3. **Enter the desired URL in the URL field.**

   If the URL you want is unavailable, a red bar will appear across the top of the page when you click into another field with a message that another person has already claimed that URL. Keep trying new URLs until you find one that is available.

4. **To make your new linked blog private, check the Password Protect This Blog check box and enter a password in the text field.**

   Otherwise, to keep this new blog public, leave the check box unchecked and the Password field blank.

5. **Click the Create Blog button to create your new linked account.**

   To exit from this page without creating a new linked account, click the Cancel button instead.

When you click the Create Blog button, the title of your new linked blog appears to the left of the Add Blog (+) button on the Tumblr Dashboard.

Depending on the number of linked accounts you create and the number of characters used in each account's title, the Add Blog icon may change to a My Blogs icon. Clicking this new button lets you toggle between your Tumblr accounts as well as add new secondary blogs to your account, as shown in Figure 4-3.

Figure 4-3: The Add Blog icon changes into a My Blogs icon when you have more than one account or long account titles.

If you want to tweak your new blog, click its title and then customize that new account:

✔ **Settings:** Click the Blog Settings button on the sidebar to add a portrait photo to the new account, as well as customize options for URL, Ask, Submissions, Facebook, Twitter, Post by Email, RSS Feeds, Language, Timezone, Directory, and Password. For details on selecting your account settings, see Chapter 1.

✔ **Members:** To add new authors or contributors to a secondary or *multi-author* blog, click the Members button on the Dashboard Sidebar. Enter the e-mail address of the first person you'd like to invite as a blog contributor and click the Invite to This Blog button. Repeat this process as needed to add members.

All blog members appear in a list on this page by profile photo and name. You can remove members from this list by clicking the Leave This Blog button next to each member's name.

Members may post as often as they like, but may not edit any of the blog's settings unless they're promoted by you to an *admin*. Admins can do everything that you can do, including removing members — and you— from the blog. Admin status may not be revoked without deleting the entire blog, so promote members with caution. Also make sure to delete members with care: If you delete the admin(s) along with all the other members, the entire blog will be removed from your account.

You may create as many new linked blogs as you like. Each new blog will appear in the Dashboard, giving you the freedom to move between them with ease.

Deleting blogs

To delete a primary blog along with any secondary blogs associated with the primary account, visit www.tumblr.com/account/delete. Alternatively, to delete only a secondary blog without altering the primary blog, click the Members button in the sidebar and click the Leave This Blog button. Tumblr automatically deletes blogs when there are no members or admins associated with it.

Searching for Help

As intuitive as Tumblr is to use, you might have a question about how a particular feature works. For those times, check out Tumblr's Help Center. You can access the Help Center page, shown in Figure 4-4, at any time by clicking the question-mark Help icon (?) on the Dashboard menu.

On the help page, you'll see a search field where you can enter a search term. Also visible is a list of frequently-asked questions and their supporting answers. For instance, if you want to know how to reset your password, the answer is "If you forget your password, you can reset it via email." Embedded within that sentence is a link to the Forgot Password page, which provides further details about how this process works.

To search for the answer to a specific question, type your question (or a keyword or two) into the How Can We Help? search field and click the blue Search button. Search results will display in a listing below the search field. Click any links within the search results to drill deeper into the answer to your inquiry.

If you ever get stuck, or can't find the exact thing you're looking for, Tumblr has you covered. When a search yields no answers, you'll see a message that says,

Sorry, we can't find that.
Please email us and we'll help you out right away.

Right below the message is a blue button labeled "Email
support@tumblr.com." Click this button to launch your
default e-mail application and e-mail your question to the folks
at Tumblr. In most cases, you'll get a reply with the answer
within 24 hours.

Search button

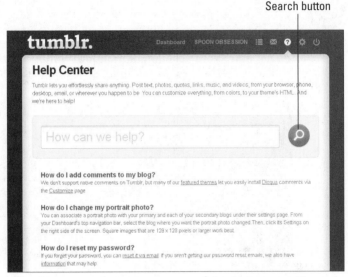

Figure 4-4: Search for help about how Tumblr works in the Help Center.

Editing Preferences

In Chapter 1, you discovered how to set your account preferences when you created your primary blog. You may edit
your preferences at any time by clicking the round spoked-
gear-shaped Preferences icon on the Dashboard menu.

From the Preferences page, you may edit your primary e-mail
address, password, post-editing mode, Dashboard options,
language, and e-mail-notification settings; if necessary, you
can also block users and delete your account. For details
about any of these options, see Chapter 1.

Logging In and Out

After you've created your primary Tumblr account (and possibly additional secondary accounts), you may log in and out of Tumblr at any time from any computer or web-enabled device.

To protect your account and keep your blog safe, be sure to look for the green "Tumblr, Inc." emblem to the left or right of your Address bar in your browser window, as shown in Figure 4-5. The exact location of the green emblem depends on your browser. If you see it, you can safely log in. If you don't see it, do not enter your account information. Without that emblem, someone could use a fake form to steal your password.

Figure 4-5: Look for the green Tumblr, Inc. emblem in your browser's address bar before logging in to your account.

Getting to Know the Sidebar

In addition to navigating your Tumblr account with the **Dashboard** menu at the top of the screen (as described in the **first part** of the chapter), you can use the context-sensitive **Dashboard** Sidebar, conveniently located on the right side of the page.

As you begin using your Tumblr account more and more, you start to see that the sidebar displays different buttons depending on where you are within your account. As shown in Figure 4-6, you have four main sidebar views:

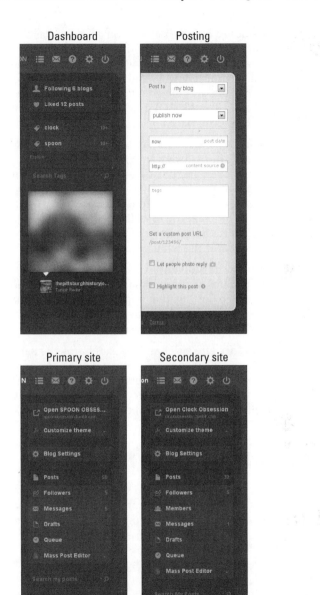

Figure 4-6: The four different Dashboard sidebars.

✔ **Dashboard sidebar:** When you click the Dashboard link at the top of your screen, the default Dashboard Sidebar displays some simple navigational buttons to help you manage your followers and likes, and to explore and search Tumblr. Below that, you'll see a random featured post from Tumblr Radar, which changes each time you visit the Dashboard.

✔ **Posting sidebar:** This sidebar with a gray background appears after clicking any of the Post type icons (text, photo, quote, and so on), and can be used to specify a handful of general posting options for each new post. If you've created any additional blogs, you will see a Post To menu at the top of the sidebar. Use this menu to select the blog where your new post will appear. For details about the features on this sidebar, see Chapter 2.

✔ **Primary site sidebar:** You can view this sidebar by clicking the name of your primary site on the Dashboard menu. The buttons that appear here help you navigate to the various pages that let you manage your account settings, posts, followers, messages, and more.

✔ **Secondary site sidebar:** This sidebar is the same as the Primary site sidebar, except it includes one additional button: Members. Click this button to invite new members to contribute to a secondary site, manage existing members, or to delete a secondary site.

Launching Your Site

Whenever you're logged in and viewing the Dashboard area, you're at the heart of your Tumblr account. However, visitors will never see this area. Instead, they'll see your actual website at the URL, *yoursite*.tumblr.com.

To launch your website from the Dashboard, follow these steps:

1. **Click the name of your primary or secondary account on the Dashboard menu.**

   This will make the Dashboard sidebar buttons appear on the right side of the screen. If your desired blog isn't listed at the top of the screen, use the My Blogs icon to select your blog from the drop-down menu.

2. **Click the Open [Your Site] button at the top of the Dashboard Sidebar.**

   Depending on your browser type, doing so opens your page in a new browser tab or browser window.

Your Tumblr website appears with your selected theme, along with any links, posts, and other theme elements you've selected. In addition, you should see two buttons in the top-right of your screen, Customize and Dashboard, as shown in Figure 4-7.

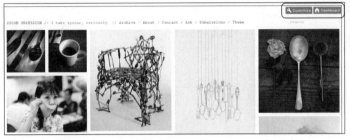

Figure 4-7: The Customize and Dashboard buttons take you back to your site's Customize Theme page or Dashboard.

When clicked, each link redirects you from the open tab or window to the respective Customize theme or Dashboard account page.

Chapter 5

Managing Posts and Messages

*N*ow that you have a basic overview of Tumblr and understand how to create posts, the next step is to find out how to manage your posts and incoming messages. In addition to editing and deleting posts through the Dashboard, this chapter provides information about how to check and respond to messages, create and save draft posts for future publishing, work with the Queue to automate your posting, and use the Mass Post Editor to make uniform changes to multiple posts all at once.

Editing and Deleting Posts

Tumblr posts are never set in stone, so if you ever make a typo, accidently forget to include (or remove!) something in your post, or simply want to go back in and change something, you can edit it at any time. In this section, you find out how to quickly and easily edit and delete your published Tumblr posts.

Keep in mind that when editing a *published* post you may not have access to every option offered when creating the *original* post. For example, some of the general posting options on the sidebar, such as Let People Photo Reply, may be absent when editing. For this reason, it's important to proofread and pre-view your posts prior to publishing (say that ten times fast!) to ensure that each one is exactly the way you want it to be.

Of course, if you really need to edit things that you can't edit, you can always copy the content from your original post into a new post and re-create it with the missing features/content. After the new post is up, the old one can be deleted.

Editing a post

To edit a published Tumblr post, follow these steps:

1. **To enter editing mode, click the name of your site at the top right of the page on the Dashboard, or select your site from the My Blogs icon menu.**

   This will show you a list of all your posts from the selected blog with the most recent post at the top of the screen.

   If needed, use your browser's scroll bars to scroll down the page until you find the post you want to edit. As you scroll down, you should see an arrow in the upper right of the browser window. Clicking that arrow will take you immediately to the top of the page.

2. **Click the gray Edit link on the right side of the post you'd like to edit.**

   When you hover your cursor over the post you'd like to edit, the top-right corner of the post shows a folded edge, as shown in Figure 5-1.

Figure 5-1: Click the Edit link on the individual post you'd like to edit.

3. **When the Edit page appears, make the changes to your post.**

   The Edit page looks similar to the original post page. You may edit the content in any text field and replace any photos, videos, or audio files with new ones. In addition to the post content itself, you may also modify the sidebar options such as content source links, tags, and the custom post URL.

4. **Click the Save Changes button when you're finished.**

   If desired, you may also click the Preview button to preview your changes before saving, or click the Cancel button to stop the editing process and return to your site's Dashboard.

Deleting a post

To delete a post from your Tumblr blog, follow these steps:

1. **To access the Delete Post feature, click the name of your site on the Dashboard or select your site from the My Blogs icon menu.**

   This displays a list of all your posts, with the most recent post at the top of the screen.

2. **Click the gray Delete link on the right side of the post you'd like to permanently delete (refer to Figure 5-1).**

3. **When the *Delete This Post?* alert box appears, click OK to delete or Cancel to return to your site's Dashboard.**

   Remember, clicking OK at this point will permanently and irreversibly remove the post from your blog. When it's gone, it's gone for good.

Reviewing Messages

Messages can come to your account mailbox from Tumblr directly when there is important news or feature updates, or from other Tumblr users in the form of questions via your site's Ask form, submissions on your Submissions page, or Fan Mail. (See Chapter 7 for more on the Ask feature, submissions, and Fan Mail.)

You will automatically see a total message count on the Messages button in the Dashboard sidebar, but you may also configure your account to display an envelope icon in the Dashboard menu by following the directions in the next section. When enabled, the envelope icon shows a red indicator when new messages arrive.

Adding the envelope icon to your Dashboard

To add the envelope icon to your Dashboard menu, you have to do two things:

1. **Open the Blog Settings page and then enable the Ask and/or Submit features. When you're finished, click Save.**

   The Blog Settings button is located in the Dashboard sidebar.

2. **Open the Preferences page and then enable the Show My Unified Inbox option. Click Save to save your changes.**

   You can access the Preferences page by clicking the gear wheel-shaped Preferences icon on the Dashboard menu.

Viewing and managing messages

To view your messages, click the envelope icon on the Dashboard menu or the Messages button on the Dashboard sidebar. Both options open the Messages page where messages appear in a listing with the most recent message at the top, as shown in Figure 5-2.

Figure 5-2: Access the Messages page by clicking the envelope icon on the Dashboard menu or the Messages button on the sidebar.

You can manage your messages in the following ways:

✔ **Answering Ask messages:** With each message, the sender's name and portrait photo appear next to the question or submission. You can click the name or photo to view the sender's Tumblr blog. You can return to your Messages page by clicking your browser's Back button.

To answer an Ask message, click the Answer link in the top-right corner of each message. This makes the sender's message expand to show a Text area where you can type your reply. When you're finished, click the Publish or Answer Privately button to send your reply.

✔ **Responding to submissions:** With *submissions* (content submitted by visitors), you may decide to publish or not publish items as you see fit. Submissions look like posts in your Dashboard, but they're unpublished and don't appear on your site until you publish them manually. See Chapter 7 for details on publishing submissions.

✔ **Replying to Fan Mail:** Fan-mail messages have a lined or tan paper background and display three icons in the bottom-right corner: a Block link, a left-facing Reply arrow, and an X to delete the message. To reply to a fan message, click the arrow icon and follow the on-screen prompts to enter and send your reply.

✔ **Blocking senders:** Should you ever get unsolicited or unsavory messages, submissions, or fan mail, you can block the sender's account, IP address, and computer by clicking the Block link next to the sender's name or at the bottom of the message.

✔ **Deleting messages:** To delete a single message, submission, or fan mail, click the delete link (X) in the top- or bottom-right corner of that message. If your Message page contains two or more messages, a Delete All button will appear on the sidebar. You can click this button to delete all the messages from your inbox at once.

Making Drafts

A *draft* is an unsent saved copy of a Tumblr post. All drafts are saved to the Drafts page, which is accessible by clicking the Drafts button on your blog's sidebar. If you don't see the Drafts button, click the name of your blog on the Dashboard menu or select it from the My Blogs icon menu.

To make a draft, create a post as you normally would, and then change the drop-down menu on the right side of the page from Publish Now to Save as Draft.

To view a list of saved drafts, click the Drafts button on the blog's sidebar. The button displays the number of drafts saved to your account. At the top of each draft in the listing, you'll see links for Delete, Edit, Queue, and Publish, as described in the following list:

✔ **Delete:** To delete a draft, click the Delete link at the top of the draft in the Drafts listing.

✔ **Edit:** Click the Edit link to open the draft and make any changes as necessary. When ready, change the drop-down menu on the sidebar from Save as Draft to Publish Now (or to one of the other publishing options).

✔ **Queue:** To move a draft to the publishing queue to be published automatically at a specific time and post frequency, click the Queue link. See the next section, "Working with the Queue," to find out more about this feature.

✔ **Publish:** You can publish your drafts one at a time by either clicking the Publish link at the top of the draft in the listing, or by clicking the Edit link first and then choosing one of the publishing options from the drop-down menu on the sidebar.

Working with the Queue

The Tumblr Queue lets you publish your posts automatically, multiple times per day, between specified hours. This tech-nique helps keep your blog active even when you're sleeping or otherwise engaged, ensuring that your visitors see a regu-lar stream of activity.

Click the Queue button on the Dashboard sidebar to view the Queue page. At the top of the page are three settings to con-trol the publishing frequency of the queued posts, as shown in Figure 5-3:

✔ **Times per day:** Select the number of times per day your blog will automatically publish posts in the Queue. The default is set to 2, and the maximum number you may select is 50.

✔ **Post between:** Queued posts are published automatically between the specified start and stop times indicated here. For example, you can choose a full 24-hour range by selecting 12:00 a.m. from the Start menu and 12:00 a.m. from the End menu.

Figure 5-3: Preview and edit posts in the Queue before they're automatically published.

Creating queued posts

Posts may be added to the Queue from a draft, new post, or existing post:

- ✓ **Drafts:** When viewing the Drafts page, you can send a draft to the Queue by clicking the Queue link at the top of each draft.

- ✓ **Posts:** When creating a new post or editing a post, select the Add to Queue option from the Publishing drop-down menu on the post's sidebar.

To modify any of the posts in the Queue before they're published, click the Queue button on the Dashboard sidebar. This opens the Queue page where each queued post is listed alongside the date and time the post will be automatically published (refer to Figure 5-3). Click the Edit link at the top of the post to modify it (see the next section for more information).

Editing queued posts

At the top of each post in the listing, you'll see links for Delete, Edit, Publish, and Reorder, which you can use to edit queued posts:

- ✔ **Delete:** To delete a queued post, click the Delete link at the top of the desired queued post.

- ✔ **Edit:** Click the Edit link to open the queued post and make any changes as necessary. When ready, click the Save Changes button to return the post to the Queue.

- ✔ **Publish:** You can publish your queued posts one at a time by either clicking the Publish link at the top of the Queue in the listing, or by clicking the Edit link first and then choosing one of the publishing options from the drop-down menu on the sidebar.

- ✔ **Reorder:** You can change the order that your queued posts will be published in by rearranging the posts within the page. To rearrange a queued post, click and drag on the post's up-/down-arrow icon to move the selected post to a new location within the page. Repeat as necessary until all posts are in the desired order.

The Queue can hold up to 300 posts at a time. If you need more space, save your additional posts as drafts until you have room to move them into your Queue.

Using the Mass Post Editor

Tumblr has a special area called the Mass Post Editor (MPE), where you may select (and unselect) multiple published posts to add or edit tags, or delete selected posts.

Open the Mass Post Editor by clicking the Mass Post Editor button on your blog's sidebar. The MPE, shown in Figure 5-4, lists the name of your site at the top of the screen along with a row of buttons that help you select and modify your posts.

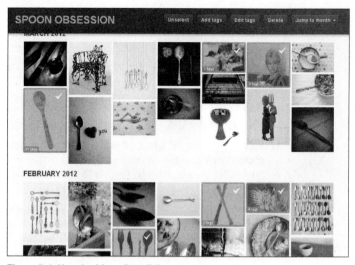

Figure 5-4: Use the Mass Post Editor to select multiple posts and then add or edit tags or delete the posts with a single command.

Follow these steps to modify multiple posts at once with the Mass Post Editor:

1. **Select all the posts you'd like to modify by clicking them one at a time.**

   Each selected post appears with a semitransparent blue overlay with a white check mark.

   To unselect all the selected posts, click the Unselect button. You may also deselect any selected posts by clicking them individually; the post is unselected when the blue overlay disappears.

2. **If needed, use the Jump to Month option to select posts in the desired month and year.**

3. **To add or edit tags, do one of the following:**

   • *Add tags:* Click the Add Tags button at the top of the screen, and in the pop-up window that appears, type in any new tags separated by commas. When finished, click the Add Tags button or click the Cancel button to return to the MPE without making any changes.

- *Edit tags:* Click the Edit Tags button at the top of the window to review the list of tags associated with your selected posts. To remove any tags in the list, click the checkbox next to each tag you'd like to delete and click the Remove Tags button. Otherwise click the Cancel button to return to the MPE.

4. **To delete all selected posts, click the Delete button.**

   A pop-up window appears, confirming the deletion. Click the OK button to delete the selected posts permanently or click the Cancel button to return to the MPE.

5. **When you're finished using the Mass Post Editor, click the name of your Tumblr blog at the top of the screen to return to your main Dashboard.**

Chapter 6

Following, Liking, and Reblogging

*T*umblr is a highly interactive blogging platform where users are encouraged to follow one another based on friendships and similar interests. In addition to following the blogs that interest you, you can *like* (that is, click an option that says you like) individual posts and reblog the posts that you want to share with your blog's followers. What's more, if you happen to have a non-Tumblr site, you can promote that content to Tumblr users by adding Tumblr share buttons to your pages. This chapter is designed to show you what you need to know about following and followers, as well as liking posts, reblogging posts, and promoting content outside of Tumblr to Tumblr users.

Following Other Blogs

One of the ways you can interact with others on Tumblr is to *follow* (subscribe to) the blogs that interest you. In fact, anyone who has a Tumblr account can follow as many Tumblr blogs as they like. That means you can follow others and others can follow you until the cows come home. Finding blogs to follow (see Chapter 8 for tips) is a fun and fascinating way to explore your interests.

Becoming a follower

After you've discovered a Tumblr blog you're interested in following, becoming a follower is as simple as clicking the Follow button, which is usually located at the top- or bottom-right side of the Tumblr blog's theme, as shown in Figure 6-1. You can track the posts of the site you're following through your Tumblr Dashboard.

Figure 6-1: Click the Follow button to follow a blog.

Viewing posts from blogs you're following

Posts from the Tumblr blogs you're following, as well as your own posts and any posts you've reblogged, are listed in the Dashboard area. At the top of each post, you'll see post details such as reblog information (who reblogged it from where), a note count (described in the next section), a link to reblog the post, and a heart icon to *like* the post (see Figure 6-2). (For more on the Like feature, see "Liking Posts," later in this chapter.)

You can tell how many blogs you're following by looking at the Following button on the Dashboard sidebar. Click the Following button to view the Following page at www.tumblr. com/following to add and remove people from that list.

Figure 6-2: Posts from Tumblr blogs you are following or have reblogged appear along with your own posts in your Dashboard page listing.

Viewing notes

Notes are the documented count of all the likes, reblogs, answers, and replies for each individual post. For example, if a lot of people have liked and reblogged a particular post, the note count may read something like 1,182 notes.

To find out more about where the blog post came from, and who else has liked and reblogged that post, click the numbered Notes link at the top of the post to toggle open the Notes Detail panel, shown in Figure 6-3. You can toggle it back closed by clicking the Notes link again.

Note details usually appear directly below the post. Each note appears with the clickable link to the name of the poster, the name of the original poster if applicable, and the reblog or Like icon. In addition, if you hover your cursor over the right side of each note, a Block link appears. Click that link only if you want to block an individual from appearing in your blog.

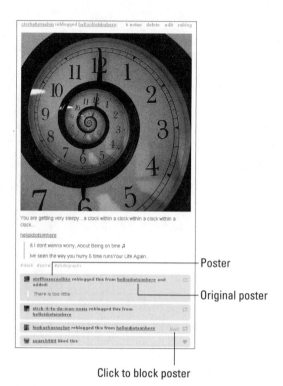

Poster

Original poster

Click to block poster

Figure 6-3: View post details by clicking the note count at the top of a post.

Managing Followers of Your Blog

When logged-in users with Tumblr accounts visit your site, they see Follow and Dashboard buttons in the upper-right corner (or sometimes in the bottom-right corner) of the screen (refer to Figure 6-1); visitors not logged in (or without Tumblr accounts), see Follow and Join Tumblr buttons. To follow your site, visitors just click the Follow button. Followers can then track the posts of your site by using their own Tumblr Dashboards.

Here are some ways that you can manage your followers:

▸ **Viewing your Followers list:** You can view a list of
your followers by clicking the Followers button on your
Dashboard sidebar. The button displays the total number
of followers, as shown in Figure 6-4. You can also see the
count on the Followers page, along with each follower's
profile photo and name.

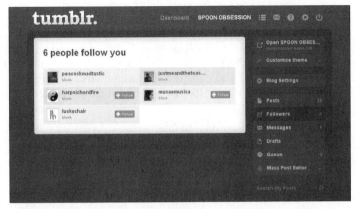

Figure 6-4: View and manage your followers on the Followers page.

▸ **Following a follower:** Each follower's name and profile
photo is a link to his or her respective website. To view a
follower's Tumblr blog, simply click the name or profile
photo.

If you want to follow one of your followers, click the
Follow button next to their name. This button disappears
after you click it.

▸ **Blocking a follower:** If you want to block a follower from
following you — thereby stopping someone from showing up on your blog and Dashboard — click the Block link
underneath the follower's name. You can also manage
blocked users and block the exact URL or username of
a tumblelog on the block page at `www.tumblr.com/`
`block`.

Liking Posts

Liking a post is the Tumblr way to tell someone that you enjoyed, agreed with, or (well, okay) liked his or her post. You can like someone's posts from your Dashboard or from within that person's Tumblr blog, and you can *unlike* any post you've liked should you ever change your mind.

Here's the lowdown on liking and unliking:

✔ **Liking from your Dashboard:** To like a post from within your Tumblr Dashboard, click the gray heart-shaped Like icon at the top of the blog post (refer to Figure 6-2). After you click the icon, the heart turns red, and a note about your liking it gets added automatically as a note to that post.

On your own blog, the like note says `You liked this`, but on everyone else's blog, the note will say `YOURNAME liked this` with a mini-version of your profile picture and a link back to your blog, as shown in Figure 6-5. That link is one of Tumblr's many ways of encouraging people to explore, network, like, and reblog each other's posts.

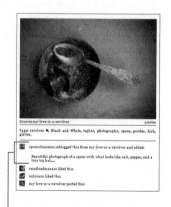

Note about your like

Figure 6-5: When you like a post, the note on the other blog includes your profile picture, blog name, and a link to your blog.

- ✔ **Liking from a blog:** To like a post directly from another person's blog, click the heart-shaped Like icon at the top of the page. If you don't see the Like icon, try clicking the blog post or blog title first. Sometimes, depending on how the theme is set up to display posts, you need to view the individual post by clicking it before you have access to the Like feature.

- ✔ **Unliking:** You can unlike a liked post at any time by clicking the heart-shaped Like icon, either from within your Dashboard or from within another person's blog. As soon as the icon turns from red to gray, any note associated with your prior like will be removed from the original post.

Reblogging Posts

If you really like a blog post by someone else, you might also want to *reblog* it simply by displaying a copy of the blog post on your own blog.

There are two ways you can reblog a post from another blog:

- ✔ **Reblogging from the Dashboard:** To reblog a post that appears on your Dashboard, click the Reblog icon at the top of the post (refer to Figure 6-2). Doing so opens the post in editing mode; there you can modify the caption, update the tags, or edit any other feature before you publish it on your own blog by clicking the Reblog Post button. To cancel the reblog before publishing, click the Cancel button.

- ✔ **Reblogging from a blog:** To reblog a post directly from another person's blog, click the Reblog link, which is typically located at the top of the page. If you don't see the Reblog link, try clicking the blog post or blog title first. Sometimes, depending on how the theme is set up to display posts, you have to select the post by clicking it before you can access the reblog feature.

  As with reblogging from within your Dashboard, clicking the Reblog button from within another blog will open the post in your Dashboard in editing mode. From there, you can modify the caption, update the tags, or edit any other feature before publishing it by clicking the Reblog Post button. Or, to cancel the reblog without publishing it, click the Cancel button.

After you reblog a post, a reblog note is added to the original post with a link back to your blog.

After you have liked and/or reblogged at least nine other posts, you (and only you) can view your nine most popular Tumblr *crushes* on your Following page at www.tumblr.com/ following. No, we're not talking the online equivalent of high school (not exactly, anyway): A *crush* is one of the nine blogs that you've most liked or most reblogged. This area, shown in Figure 6-6, is constantly updated to reflect your personal Tumblr activity.

Figure 6-6: View your Tumblr crushes on the Following page.

Adding Tumblr Share Buttons to a Non-Tumblr Site

Did you know that there are over 13 million Tumblr bloggers with over 48 million Tumblr blogs around the world? It's true, and these numbers are constantly growing. So if you happen to have another website outside of Tumblr, you might be unintentionally passing up the chance to interact with the Tumblr audience.

One reason the Tumblr community is so strong is that Tumblr posts are so easily shared and reblogged among Tumblr users. So what does that mean for websites that aren't connected to Tumblr?

Fortunately, the folks at Tumblr have already thought about this for you and have devised a way to help you promote your non-Tumblr website content to everyone on Tumblr. All you need to do to make those pages Tumblr-friendly is to add a few strategically placed custom Tumblr buttons.

It's pretty easy to grab the button code to add a variety of Tumblr share buttons to your non-Tumblr site. Just follow these steps:

1. **Open the Tumblr Button page at** www.tumblr.com/ docs/en/share_button, **as shown in Figure 6-7.**

   This is where you can get a copy of the code you'll need.

Figure 6-7: Add Tumblr share buttons to your non-Tumblr websites.

2. **Select and copy the line of** `<script>` **code in the gray area and paste it into your pages right before the closing** `</body>` **tag.**

   If you're familiar with HTML and have access to all the code, you could place this script code before the closing `</head>` tag instead.

3. **Build a custom Tumblr button for your page by selecting either the Basic or Advanced option and then selecting the button you want to add to your site.**

   Use the Basic option to grab the code for a simple share button. The Advanced option, by contrast, lets you embed the Tumblr button inside a link, pull quote, photo, or video, as well as choose the programming language: PHP, Ruby on Rails, or JavaScript.

   The Share button code in the Share Button Code text field updates automatically to match the button you select.

4. **If you selected the Advanced option in Step 3, select the desired option under Share As and choose a programming language from the drop-down menu.**

5. **Select all the code in the Share Button Code text field.**

   Make sure you select all the code from the starting to closing tags.

6. **Paste the code into the desired location within the HTML of your non-Tumblr website.**

   You may paste this same code into your pages as many times as desired — in as many pages as desired.

7. **Save the changes to your updated non-Tumblr pages and upload the pages to your remote host server.**

   When the pages are in place on the remote server, you should see the Tumblr buttons. If not, go back and check your code to ensure that you've added it correctly.

After the buttons appear on your site, any Tumblr users who happen to view your pages can easily click the Tumblr Share button to share your content on their Tumblr blogs.

Chapter 7

Interacting with Others

- -

In This Chapter

▶ Asking and answering questions

▶ Making and accepting submissions

▶ Sending and receiving Fan Mail

▶ Attending Meetups

- -

Many Tumblr users will agree, there's nothing better than checking your posts to see how many other Tumblr visitors have liked and reblogged something from your site. By far, this is one of the main reasons that so many people love using Tumblr.

Interacting with others is at the heart of Tumblr's success. In addition to exploring Tumblr to find photos, GIF animations, quotes, videos, and music shared by others to reblog yourself, you can ask other users questions, submit to each others' blogs, reply to inquiries, send each other Fan Mail, and even attend official Tumblr Meetups to meet — in person — other like-minded Tumblr enthusiasts. By the end of this chapter, you'll know how to interact with others on Tumblr.

Asking and Answering Questions

For every Tumblr site you create, you have the option of allowing visitors to ask you questions. For instance, someone might want to know more about you or your skills and services, or have a question about something you posted. Once their question arrives in your mailbox, you have the option of answering it as a post on your blog or answering it as a message in private.

Enabling the Ask feature

To add the Ask feature on your Tumblr blog, follow these steps:

1. **Click the name of your Tumblr blog on the Dashboard.**

2. **Click the Blog Settings button on the Dashboard sidebar.**

3. **On the Blog Settings page, put a check mark in the Ask field where it says Let People Ask Questions.**

   Enabling this feature adds an Ask link to your blog's navigation menu that, when clicked, sends visitors to *yoursite*/tumblr/ask.

4. **If desired, edit the Ask page title in the text field provided.**

   The default title is Ask me anything.

5. **To allow visitors to submit anonymous questions without having to provide their names and e-mail addresses, put a check mark in the Allow Anonymous Questions box.**

   You also need to click the OK button in the warning box that appears. Giving your visitors anonymity is risky and can bring out the worst in people. In other words, although anonymity might seem like a cool idea, don't think twice about disabling this feature in the future if you need to.

6. **Scroll down to the bottom of the page and click the Save button.**

   Upon saving, Tumblr will create your new Ask page and add it to your site at *yoursite*.tumblr.com/ask. Be patient; sometimes it takes a few minutes for the page to appear.

After enabling this feature on your blog, visitors will see the Ask option somewhere in your blog's navigation, as a graphic link, or elsewhere on the page, according to the specifications of your blog's theme. Figure 7-1 shows two examples of how the Ask option might appear on a Tumblr blog.

Click to open Ask page

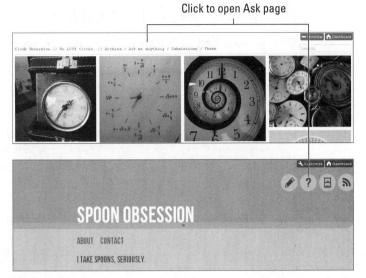

Figure 7-1: The Ask feature usually displays in your navigation menu (top) or as a clickable graphic icon (bottom).

Asking a question

To ask a question, all visitors need to do is click the Ask link to be taken to the Ask page where they can type in and submit their question. Figure 7-2 shows an example of a typical Ask page, which is often quite plain, containing a simple text box and Ask button.

Figure 7-2: To ask a question, simply fill out the Ask form and submit.

Answering a question

On your own blog, anytime someone asks you a question, a message will appear in your Inbox. On the Messages page, shown in Figure 7-3, each message appears as a separate post including the sender's name and portrait photo next to their question.

Figure 7-3: Incoming messages appear on your Messages page.

You can answer, ignore, delete, or block messages:

✔ **Answering messages:** To answer a message, click the Answer link in the top-right corner of the message box. The message area expands to show a text area where you can type your reply. When finished, click the Publish or Answer Privately button to send your reply.

✔ **Ignoring messages:** To ignore a message, simply leave it in your Inbox indefinitely or delete it without responding to the sender.

✔ **Deleting messages:** To delete a message from your Messages page, click the delete (X) link at the top-right of the message box.

✔ **Blocking messages:** To block a particular sender from sending you any additional messages, click the message's Block link.

Creating question posts

Asking other people questions or having them ask you questions is great in most cases. But what if you want to ask your followers a specific question? Tumblr has the perfect solution, which most Tumblr users don't know about. It's called Question posts.

A Question post lets you turn a regular post into a post that invites and collects answers from anyone on the Internet — both Tumblr users and non-Tumblr users alike.

To create a Question post, simply end your text or caption with a question mark (?), and if the post type allows it, select the Let People Answer This option in the post Dashboard sidebar. The option that lets people reply automatically appears after the post is published to your blog. If desired, you can also enable the option in the sidebar that lets people photo reply to your question post. You can create Question posts for any Text, Photo, Link, Audio, or Video post. Figure 7-4 shows an example of how a text Question post might look to visitors.

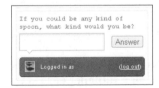

Figure 7-4: Question posts let you directly ask questions of your site's visitors.

Making and Accepting Submissions

Sites that showcase information gathered from other visitors can get their post content in two ways. They can reblog posts directly from other sites, and they can ask visitors to submit photos, text, chats, quotes, audio, and video files using Tumblr's built-in Submission form.

Enabling the Submit feature

To enable the Submit feature on your blog, follow these steps:

1. **Click the name of your Tumblr blog on the Dashboard menu.**

2. **Click the Blog Settings button on the Dashboard sidebar to view the Settings page.**

3. **Put a check mark in the Submit field where it says Let People Submit Posts.**

   Enabling this feature adds a Submit link to your blog's navigation menu that is linked to your site's Submit page: *yoursite*/tumblr/submit.

4. **If desired, edit the Submit page title in the text field provided.**

   The default title is Submit.

5. **In the Submission Guidelines field, enter any instructions to visitors about making submissions.**

   For instance, you may want to specify a maximum width and height for photo submissions or suggest that visitors include a click-through link for the source of any content they submit.

6. **In the Allowed Post Types area, select which types of posts your visitors may submit.**

   The options are Text, Photo, Quote, Link, and Video. You may select as many of these options as you like.

7. **To include a set of optional tags that visitors can include with their submissions, enter the tags in the Optional Tags for Submitter field.**

   To enter multiple tags, be sure to separate each word or phrase from the others with a comma and a space, as in: spoon, spoons, silver, wood, paper, plastic, metal, and so on, as shown in Figure 7-5.

Figure 7-5: Enable the Submit feature on your Settings page to accept post submissions on your blog.

8. Click Save to save your changes.

After you enable the Submit feature on your blog, visitors will see the Submit option somewhere in your blog's navigation as a text or graphic link, or elsewhere on the page, according to the specifications of your blog's theme. You can also access the page directly at `http://yoursite.tumblr.com/submit`.

Be sure to check your new Submit page for typographical errors and readability. If needed, return to the Settings page to adjust your Submission Guidelines text and other settings.

Submitting to a site

To submit a post to another site, click the site's Submission link and complete the Submission form, providing all the information requested. If multiple post types are allowed, you may need to select your desired type through the Post Type drop-down menu at the top of the submission form area, shown in Figure 7-6. Upon receipt of your submission, the site's administrator will determine whether (and when) to publish your submission.

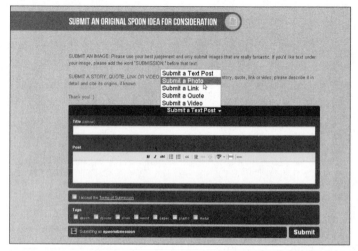

Figure 7-6: Submit information to another blog using the Submit page form.

Responding to a submission

After a visitor submits a post to your site, a message appears in your Inbox, and you can choose whether to publish, ignore, or delete the submission as you see fit.

Incoming submissions, like those shown in Figure 7-7, appear on your Messages page as individual unpublished posts. Each post includes the submitter's name and Tumblr account portrait photo. To check out the submitter's Tumblr blog, click the name or profile photo associated with the submission. You can return to the Messages page by clicking your browser's Back button.

Submission

Figure 7-7: Submissions appear in your Dashboard Inbox as unpublished posts that only you can see.

Incoming submissions can be queued, published, blocked, ignored, edited, or deleted:

- ✔ **Queue submissions:** To put a submission directly into your Queue for automatic publishing, click the Queue link at the top of the post.

- ✔ **Publish submissions:** To convert an unpublished submission into a published post on your blog, click the Publish link.

- ✔ **Block submissions:** To block a person from sending you additional submissions, click the post's Block link. You can unblock a sender, if needed, on the Block Tumblelogs page at www.tumblr.com/block.

- ✔ **Ignore submissions:** While not the best netiquette, you can choose to ignore a message by simply leaving it in your Inbox indefinitely or deleting it without responding to the sender.

✔ **Edit submissions:** When you click the Edit link, the post opens in Edit mode. In editing mode, you can modify the submission content as desired and change the publishing status in the right sidebar area from Unapproved to Publish Now or to one of the other publishing options, as described in Chapter 2. When you're finished, click the Save Post button, or click Cancel to return the post submission to Unpublished status on your Messages page.

✔ **Delete submissions:** To delete a submission entirely from your Messages page, click the delete (X) link at the top-right of the submission post.

Sending and Receiving Fan Mail

Fan Mail, which made its debut on Tumblr in January 2012, is the most recent addition to Tumblr's roster of fun ways to interact with others. The goal of this feature is to give Tumblr users a way to send fan mail to their favorite blogs. Figure 7-8 shows the post that Tumblr sent out to all its users announcing the news about this new feature.

Figure 7-8: Fan Mail was conceived as a way to share your appreciation with the blogs you follow.

Sadly, as with most good things, some people have already found unsavory and spammy ways to abuse this nifty tool. For the majority of us, however, Fan Mail remains a fun and fresh way to share our genuine appreciation of one another.

Sending Fan Mail

To send an appreciative Fan Mail message to a blog you admire, follow these steps:

1. **Access the Send Fan Mail page from any of the following locations, as shown in Figure 7-9:**

    *   *Inbox:* Click the blue Send Fan Mail button that displays on your Dashboard sidebar after clicking the Messages button.

    *   *Blog icon:* Many themes include a Fan Mail envelope icon next to the Unfollow and Dashboard buttons. If you see it, click the tiny envelope icon in the top-right corner of any blog you're following.

    *   *Avatar info menu:* From your Dashboard, hover your cursor over a profile photo next to any of the posts of the blogs you're following. When you see a tiny "i" (for info) inside a circle appear on the lower-left corner of the photo, click the circle and select the Fan Mail option from the drop-down menu.

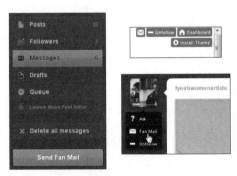

Figure 7-9: Send Fan Mail from your Inbox, a blog envelope icon, or an avatar info drop-down menu.

The Fan Mail message window appears, as shown in Figure 7-10.

Figure 7-10: The Fan Mail message window opens on top of the page you're viewing, appearing as a darkened window overlay.

2. **In the Send To field, enter the name of the blog you want to send mail to.**

   For example, to send a message to a blog at spoon obsession.tumblr.com, enter **spoonobsession** in the Send To field.

3. **Place your cursor inside the large text area and type your message.**

   Share the love. Let your recipients know why you like their sites and how much you appreciate them taking the time to post the things they do. Tell them a little about yourself or share a funny story or joke, if it makes sense to do so; it's up to you.

   If it looks like you're running out of room, don't worry and keep typing. You can use the up/down arrows on your keyboard to reveal the hidden areas of your message.

4. **If you have more than one blog, use the drop-down menu at the bottom of the message area to choose which blog account you'd like to send your message from.**

Your primary account is listed at the top of the drop-down menu, with secondary accounts listed below that.

5. **If desired, select one of the two paper types listed in the Paper area to the right of your message.**

   As of this writing, there are two options: lined paper and parchment.

6. **You may also select a font from the Writing section to the right of your message.**

   As this book is written, there are three font options: serif (left), handwriting (center), and sans-serif (right).

7. **Click the Send button to send your Fan Mail.**

   Upon clicking Send, you briefly see a Sent! alert on the screen before you're returned to the page you were on before sending the message.

   To discard your message and close the Fan Mail message window without sending, click the Cancel button. If you don't see a Cancel button (which happens sometimes when you click the blog icon as described in Step 1), click your browser's Back button.

Receiving Fan Mail

As soon as someone sends you a message, Fan Mail goes right to your Inbox. A Fan Mail message looks like a regular post in your Inbox, but it has a lined-paper or parchment-paper background. The message also shows the sender's avatar (profile photo) and name. If you want, you can reply to the sender by clicking the little arrow icon at the bottom of the message.

When you're finished reading your Fan Mail, you can leave it in your Inbox indefinitely, or click the X at the bottom of the message to delete it.

At this time, Tumblr doesn't have any way for you to save or archive your Fan Mail separately from the rest of your messages, but if that's a feature you think you'd like, send the folks at Tumblr a quick note with your suggestion to suggestions@tumblr.com.

Attending Meetups

Remarkably, Tumblr users from all around the world are getting together to meet in person at *Meetups*. A Meetup is a public event organized by a group of Tumblr users who have shared interests.

You can find out if there are any upcoming scheduled Meetups near you on the Tumblr website. If there aren't, you might want to consider organizing your own Tumblr Meetup. Tumblr can even help you spread the word to people in your general geographic region.

Attending a Tumblr Meetup

To view a listing of upcoming scheduled Meetups around the world, visit the Tumblr Meetups page at www.tumblr.com/meetups. Meetups are scheduled by date, city, meeting location, and time, with the soonest meetings listed at the top of the page, as shown in Figure 7-11.

Figure 7-11: Join other Tumblr enthusiasts in your area at a local Tumblr Meetup!

If you see a Meetup location that you'd like to join, click it to view that Meetup's details. From there, you can view location details, RSVP in the top-right corner of the page, and add any comments to that Meetup's discussion board. Then all you need to do is put the date on your own calendar and show up. The rest is up to you.

Scheduling a Tumblr Meetup

Each Tumblr Meetup acts as its own entity where members can choose how many members to have, where and when to meet, and make other group-related decisions. What's more, groups can contact Tumblr directly to get help organizing a Meetup and request a free kit that includes stickers and name-tags from http://tumblr.com/meetups/organize.

It might take a few weeks to get everything ready for your first local Meetup, such as getting your kit, choosing a venue, sending out invites, and being listed on the Tumblr Meetup schedule. After you've held your first meeting, however, subsequent meetings should take only a few days to get listed on the Tumblr site. The folks at Tumblr want to support you in your efforts, so if you need assistance with scheduling or cancelling a meeting, or have a Meetup-related question, you may e-mail them directly at meetups@tumblr.com.

For examples of fun Meetup ideas, locations, and event activities, and to learn more about Meetups in general, visit the Tumblr Meetups blog at http://meetups.tumblr.com/.

Chapter 8

Exploring Tumblr

. . . .

In This Chapter

▶ Searching by tags

▶ Exploring Tumblr by category

▶ Exploring sites in Tumblr's Spotlight

▶ Finding people on Tumblr

▶ Discovering Tumblr Goodies

. . . .

*T*he world of Tumblr is an amazing mishmash of global content that spans a wide variety of topics from general interest to the obscure. You'll find thousands and thousands of sites about art, illustration, photography, history, tattoos, comics, animals, design, nail art, gaming, sports, celebs, fashion, DIY, LGBTQ, NFL, LOL, robots, literature, poetry, tech, politics, education, news, and more!

Chances are you can find information about anything you can conceive of on Tumblr. There are even several different ways to search through Tumblr including searching by tags, by category, or by a person's name or blog title. In addition, Tumblr offers you some free and fun Goodies to help enhance your Tumblogging experience.

This chapter shows you how to search by tags and keywords, explore all the features in Tumblr's Spotlight, and discover how you can use features like free bookmarklets and audio posting on Tumblr's Goodies page.

Searching by Tags

Searching Tumblr is probably half the fun of using it, and one of the fastest ways to find blogs on a particular topic is to use the Search Tags feature on the Dashboard sidebar. The Search field lets you toggle between four different search options using the magnifying glass icon, as shown in Figure 8-1:

- ✔ **Search Tags:** This option lets you search for tags throughout the Tumblverse.

- ✔ **My Dashboard:** Use this option to search for tags on your own posts and any of the blogs you follow.

- ✔ **My Posts:** This search option limits your tag search to just the content inside your own posts.

- ✔ **Help Docs:** Use this option to access Tumblr's Help Center, where you can search for answers about a particular keyword or feature.

Search field

Figure 8-1: Choose the Search Tags option to search Tumblr for specific tags, keywords, or key phrases.

To search Tumblr for a particular tag, follow these steps:

1. **In the Search field on the Dashboard sidebar, enter a tag or keyword.**

   For best results, enter only a single word or phrase, such as "Mario" or "chocolate chip cookies" rather than a list of words separated by commas.

2. **If needed, select the Search Tags option from the search field drop-down menu (refer to Figure 8-1).**

You may also choose to search your Dashboard, your posts, or the help docs.

3. Press Enter/Return to initiate the search.

Your search results appear in the center of the page in a long list of posts from all over the world. If no results are found that match your search, the words No posts found appear on the screen.

4. Explore your search results.

If you find any posts you enjoy, you can Like and Reblog them by clicking the Reblog link and heart icon at the top of each post (see Chapter 7 for details).

Notice the new Track button that appears on your sidebar, like the one shown in Figure 8-2? Any time you search for a tag, Tumblr gives you the option of saving that search as a Track button by clicking that button's Track link.

Figure 8-2: Create Track buttons to follow topics by tag. _____

After it's saved, the button remains on your sidebar and displays a little tag icon to the left of the tag name. Each Track button lets you follow topics without adding posts to your Dashboard. For as long as you like, the button stays visible on your dashboard sidebar, quietly tracking and counting all new posts that have that tag. Then, any time you want to see the new posts on that topic, you can click that Track button to view the results. This button is especially helpful if you like to reblog posts on a particular topic.

You can create as many Track buttons as you like, as well as delete any Track button from your sidebar by clicking the button to select it, and then clicking that button's X icon.

Exploring Tumblr by Category

Another fun way to explore Tumblr is to search by category on Tumblr's Explore page at www.tumblr.com/explore. The page is divided into two parts, a category grid at the top and a more detailed listing at the bottom, as shown in Figure 8-3. Depending on your personal preferences, you may enjoy exploring Tumblr through one method more than the other.

Category of the post

Figure 8-3: Have fun exploring popular tags on Tumblr's Explore page.

Exploring the Wire

At the top of the Explore page, you'll see a grid of 18 boxes, which Tumblr calls the *Wire*. Each box represents a popular search category that you might be interested in exploring, such as Architecture or Food. Inside each square, you'll see a static or animated picture or quote pulled from a Tumblr post related to that category. In addition, each box includes a tag in the bottom-left corner that identifies the category the post belongs in (refer to Figure 8-3).

If you happen to look at the page for more than a minute or two, you'll notice that each row shifts slightly to the right, revealing a new square. This feature helps keep the content in the Wire fresh, exposing you to new ideas and information.

To view the posts associated with any category in the Wire, click the square that interests you. From there, you'll be transferred to your Dashboard where you can explore a listing of related posts.

If you find any posts you enjoy, you can Like and Reblog them by clicking the Reblog link and heart icon at the top of each post.

In addition to exploring the listings, you'll also see a temporary category Track button in your sidebar, like the one shown in Figure 8-4. Also in your sidebar, you see links to popular editors and contributors within that category. To save the Track button for that tag for future reference, click the button's Track link.

Figure 8-4: After you click a box on the Wire, a temporary Track button appears on your sidebar along with links to popular editors and contributors.

Exploring by listing

Directly below the Wire on Tumblr's Explore page, you'll find a listing of some of the most popular tags searched for on Tumblr's site, as shown in Figure 8-5. You may prefer to explore Tumblr from this listing instead of from the Wire, because you can learn more about each tag's popularity before viewing a list of posts.

Figure 8-5: You can also explore Tumblr by using the sortable Explore page Popular Tags listing.

Here are some ways you can explore the list of popular tags:

✔ **Change the sort order of a column:** You can click any of the column headers (except Top Editor) to re-sort the listing by popular tags, feedback, and activity. You can tell at a glance how the whole list is sorted by the presence and direction of a small arrow next to one of the column headers.

Tags can be sorted in alphabetical or reverse alphabetical order, while the Feedback and Activity columns can be sorted from most to least or least to most.

The Feedback column represents the amount of feedback received, while the Activity column shows a set of 15 green bars, which represent the amount of Activity for that tag over the past 15 days. If you want, you can even hover your cursor over the green bars to reveal which day each bar represents.

✔ **Explore a category:** If you see a category you'd like to explore further, click a tag name to view a listing of recent posts on that topic. The tag name will then appear as a potential Track button in your sidebar. To save a Track button for future reference, click the button's Track link.

✔ **View an editor's recent posts:** You can click the name of the editor in the Top Editor column to view that editor's recent posts (which are usually reblogs). The editors in this list are people who are preselected by TumblrBot based on post relevance and popularity. Contributors, by contrast, are Tumblr bloggers whose posts are repeatedly selected by editors.

Checking Out Sites Featured on Spotlight

Another interesting place to discover the new and the unusual on Tumblr is the Spotlight at www.tumblr.com/spotlight.

The Spotlight page features sites that the folks at Tumblr find interesting, so you know they've got to be good. As you can see in Figure 8-6, the Spotlight page is organized into three columns that feature Tumblr sites in the spotlight, and a fourth column that lists popular categories in alphabetical order. You can click any of the categories to view the sites featured there.

Grabbing the Spotlight

Tumblr claims that a "Tumblrbot" — which may or may not be a computer algorithm — determines which Tumblr members will be included into the Spotlight. If you think your site deserves to be featured in one of their categories, you can send them an e-mail at editors@tumblr.com with your blog URL and the category you're interested in being in. Good luck!

Each featured site on this page shows a photograph, the site title, a brief bio, and in most cases the geographic location of the site's origin. Click anywhere inside a rectangle to visit that Tumblr blog in your browser.

If you hover your cursor above any of the featured sites on this page, a Follow button appears on top of the photo. You can click the button to follow a site without viewing it. To unfollow it, however, you need to visit the site itself to click the Unfollow button there.

Figure 8-6: Find inspiration and creativity on Tumblr's Spotlight page.

Searching for People on Tumblr

With a little bit of poking around on Tumblr, you're virtually guaranteed to find at least one other person you know who's already part of the Tumblr community.

Finding people using your address book

There are a few different ways you can search for people on Tumblr, but perhaps the easiest way is to start with your

Gmail or Yahoo! address book. To find out if anyone you already know is on Tumblr in your Gmail or Yahoo! address book, follow these steps:

1. **Open the Tumblr Lookup page in your browser at** `www.tumblr.com/lookup`.

   You can also access this page by clicking the Following button on the Dashboard sidebar, and then selecting the People You Know tab at the top of the page.

2. **Click the icon for the e-mail account you'd like to access.**

   Current support is limited to Gmail and Yahoo! e-mail accounts.

3. **In the new browser window or tab that opens, sign in to your e-mail account by entering your e-mail address/ID and password.**

   If you're already signed in to your e-mail account, skip ahead to Step 4.

   Your browser may prompt you to save your password. If you're on your own computer, that's probably fine. If, however, you're using a public computer or a computer that you share with others, you may choose not to have the browser remember your password.

4. **Tumblr then requests permission for you to allow access to your e-mail account's contacts. Click the Allow Access or Agree button to proceed.**

   To cancel the request, click the No Thanks button or Sign Out at the top of the page.

   You may need to wait a moment or two while the account "awaits authorization" as it synchronizes the address book with Tumblr. Tumblr then displays a list of Tumblr sites with e-mail addresses that match people in your address book. Each match is listed by profile photo, Tumblr title, and e-mail address, as shown in Figure 8-7.

   If there are not matches between your address book and Tumblr, a message will appear that says `No Friends Found`.

Figure 8-7: Check your Gmail and Yahoo! e-mail accounts to see whether anyone you know is on Tumblr.

5. To view the Tumblr site of anyone in your listing, click the profile photo or blog name.

You may also click the Follow button to follow someone without viewing the associated Tumblr blog.

After you establish a Tumblr link with your e-mail account, click the appropriate e-mail icon on this page to refresh the listing. Any new e-mail accounts that have been added to your address book since you first scanned it that match a Tumblr account will be added to the address book listing on this page.

Adding people to follow manually

Another quick and easy way to add people to your "list of Tumblr sites to follow" is to use the Follow Form at www. tumblr.com/following. You can also get to this page by clicking the Following button on the Dashboard sidebar.

The page displays a simple Follow Form at the top of the screen, followed by a listing of all the sites you're currently following, as shown in Figure 8-8.

Figure 8-8: Add people to follow on Tumblr's Following page.

For each person listed, you'll see a mini profile photo, the name of the blog, a note indicating the last time that person updated their Tumblr site, and an Unfollow button. You can view any of the sites in the list by clicking the name or profile photo. To unfollow someone, click the Unfollow button to the right of the profile name.

You can add people to your Following list by entering their Tumblr URL, username, or e-mail address in the search field provided and clicking the Follow button.

Tumblr displays a message at the top of the screen (as shown in Figure 8-9) to let you know whether the search term was found:

- ✔ If Tumblr locates the person or Tumblr account you're searching for, a green message appears at the top of the page that says Added *Name*. You may then click the underlined name to view that Tumblr blog.

- ✔ If you enter a name, URL, or e-mail address that cannot be found, a red error message appears that says Sorry, we couldn't find that tumblelog on Tumblr.

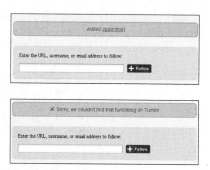

Figure 8-9: A green message appears when Tumblr locates someone (top); a red message means Tumblr can't find the URL, username, or e-mail address (bottom).

Discovering Tumblr's Goodies

The folks at Tumblr like to take care of their users by providing fun ways to improve their Tumblr experience. To that end, they've developed (and continue to develop) a whole page full of cool Goodies for you to choose from including a free bookmarklet, info about Tumblr for your phone, tips on backing up your blog, making audio posts, and more.

The Goodies page is located at www.tumblr.com/goodies. You can also access this page by clicking the Goodies link in the footer of most Tumblr pages.

Using Tumblr's Bookmarklet

A *bookmarklet* is a free little browser widget that you can drag onto your browser's Bookmarks toolbar (or Favorites toolbar in Internet Explorer) to share content on your Tumblr blog that you find while surfing the Internet.

To start using the bookmarklet in your browser, locate the bookmarklet section of the Goodies page and drag the gray Share on Tumblr button to your browser's bookmarks bar, as shown in Figure 8-10. The option to make your Bookmarks toolbar visible varies by browser type, so check your browser's Help area for details.

Figure 8-10: Add the free Tumblr bookmarklet to your browser's Bookmarks Bar.

After you add the bookmarklet to your Bookmarks toolbar, click it to share content from another site on your Tumblr page. Here's how it works:

1. **Find a page on the Internet that has content you want to share on your Tumblr.**

   The content can include text, a photo, a quote, a link, a chat, or a video.

2. **Click the Share on Tumblr bookmarklet button on your browser's Bookmarks toolbar.**

   This opens a mini Share on Tumblr pop-up browser window containing a post form you can complete to submit the content to your Tumblr site, as shown in Figure 8-11.

Figure 8-11: Complete the form inside the Share on Tumblr pop-up window to share content from other sites on your Tumblr page.

3. **Select the post type from the tabs at the top of the page.**

   Tab options are Text, Photo, Quote, Link, Chat, and Video.

4. **Complete the form for the post type you selected.**

   For example, if you selected Photo, enter a caption and select the photo you want to post from a list of images found on the website.

5. **(Optional) Click the Advanced tab to set any additional publishing options.**

   Settings here include options to set the publishing time, a click-through link, the post date, tags for the post, and a custom URL. To return to the main post area, click the Advanced tab again.

6. **If you have one or more secondary blogs, choose the blog you'd like to publish to from the drop-down menu at the bottom of the pop-up window.**

   The menu shows your primary Tumblr account name by default.

7. Click the Create Post button.

This will send the post to your blog and automatically close the pop-up window for you.

Pretty slick, right? Use this bookmarklet to share content on your Tumblr blog as often as you like.

Installing Tumblr for your phone

Next up on the Goodies page is a section about Tumblr for your phone. Currently you can find apps here for your iPhone, Blackberry, and Android (OS 2.1+) device.

To find out more about how to install your phone's Tumblr app, click the link that matches your phone type (refer to Figure 8-10):

- ✔ **iPhone:** There are three ways to get Tumblr on your device: by searching for "tumblr" in the App Store, by having a download link e-mailed to you, or by opening it in iTunes.

- ✔ **Blackberry:** If you're a Blackberry user, you can search for "tumblr" in App World, have a download link e-mailed to you, or get a direct download.

- ✔ **Android:** If you own an Android phone, you can install Tumblr from the Google Play (formerly the Android Market) or scan a barcode with your phone.

When you're finished reviewing your phone's download options, click the small X in the top-left corner of the pop-up screen or simply click away from the screen to return to your main browser window.

Backing up your blog

At the time of this writing, Tumblr is beta-testing a new backup/exporting application for Mac OS X. You can download the Mac software from the Goodies page by clicking the Backup Your Blog link, shown in Figure 8-12.

Figure 8-12: Tumblr is currently beta-testing a backup tool for Mac OS X.

With the Tumblr Backup tool, you can log in to your account, select the blog you'd like to back up (if you have more than one), choose your Save To destination, and create the backup.

A Windows version of the same tool, according to their website, is "coming soon."

Linking to Facebook

If you haven't already linked your Tumblr account to your Facebook page in your Tumblr blog's Settings page, you can do it from the Goodies page by clicking the Facebook Application link (refer to Figure 8-12). The browser takes you to a Facebook login screen where you may enter your Facebook account credentials.

If, for some reason, you get an error message that says, `Sorry, the application you were using is misconfigured. Please try again later,` simply open your Blog Settings page by clicking the button of that name on your Dashboard and configure your account settings there.

Publishing to Twitter

In addition to sharing your Tumblr posts on Facebook, you can also tweet them on Twitter, which is a nice way to keep all your social media accounts in sync.

You can connect Tumblr to Twitter by signing in to your Twitter account on your Tumblr blog's Blog Settings page.

 Another way to connect your accounts works only if your Tumblr theme supports Twitter account input in the Appearance section of the Customize Theme page. To see if your theme supports this feature, click the Publish to Twitter link on the Goodies page (refer to Figure 8-12). This will open your browser to the Customize Theme page. If you see a place to enter your Twitter name in the Appearance section, enter it, click the Save button, and then click the Close button to return to your Dashboard.

Audio posting by telephone

Question: Quick! You're away from your computer and other web-enabled devices, and you need to post something on your Tumblr blog. What will you do?

Answer: Tumblr has you covered! The answer is . . . create an Audio post from your phone.

To configure your Tumblr account to accept audio posts by phone, follow these steps:

1. **Click the Configure button in the Call In Audio section of the Goodies page (refer to Figure 8-12).**

   This expands the area on the page so you can enter some data.

2. **Make a note of the toll-free telephone number listed here.**

   If needed, change the country code to match your calling location.

3. **Enter your phone number in the field provided.**

   Be sure to include your area code and/or non-U.S. country codes.

4. **(Optional) For security, type in a 1-to-4-digit PIN code.**

   Write it down or commit it to memory!

5. **If you have more than one blog, select the name of your blog from the drop-down menu under "Blog to post to."**

6. **Click the Save button to save your audio call settings.**

To test the configuration, create your first audio post. Call the toll-free number and enter your PIN number if prompted. Then talk into the phone to create your audio post. When you're finished speaking, simply hang up. Your audio post appears on your Tumblr Dashboard page, along with a little audio bar that says `Click to play`, as shown in Figure 8-13. How it looks on your Tumblr blog depends on your theme's settings.

Audio post

Figure 8-13: Creating audio posts by phone is a fun and convenient way to keep your Tumblr blog fresh.

If needed you may edit your audio post by clicking the Edit button on the post in your Dashboard. Or, if you hate the recording and want to try again, click the Delete link to delete the post from your blog. You can also edit your phone settings by returning to the Goodies page and deleting or changing the phone number and PIN.

Embedding your blog on another webpage

Did you know that you can include your Tumblr blog feed inside another web page? Yup! However, Tumblr recommends this feature only for advanced users who are comfortable coding in HTML and CSS.

To add your Tumblr to another web page, follow these steps:

1. **Copy the script code provided in the text field located in the Embed Your Blog section of the Goodies page (refer to Figure 8-12).**

   The code will look something like this, with the word *yoursite* replaced with the name of your Tumblr site:

   ```
   <script type="text/javascript"
   src="http://yoursite.tumblr.com/js">
   </script>
   ```

2. **Paste the code into the body of the web page where you'd like your Tumblr content to appear.**

3. **Create any new CSS styles as needed to skin the HTML, save your file, and upload it to your host server.**

   For additional technical help, visit Tumblr's API docs page at www.tumblr.com/docs/en/api/v2.

Chapter 9

Discovering, Modifying, and Designing Themes

. . . .

In This Chapter

▶ Finding and installing themes from the Theme Garden

▶ Modifying the HTML for a theme

▶ Creating your own theme and submitting it to Tumblr

▶ Exploring online theme tutorials

. . . .

*I*f the eyes are a window to the soul, think of your Tumblr theme as the favorite outfit you wear when you go out for a night on the town. You want to look sharp, be attractive to the right audience, and let people know more about you by the flavor of your ensemble. In other words, your Tumblr theme shouldn't just sit there, it should do something; it should tell your visitors — visually — more about who you are and what you like, and hopefully complement the kinds of content that you post on your site.

As of now, 1,275 free and premium themes are featured in the Tumblr Theme Garden, and that number is growing daily. In addition, there are hundreds of other themes available, for free and for a fee, directly from developers' websites. In this chapter, you discover how to explore and use Tumblr's Theme Garden. You then find out how to install and customize themes and edit a theme's HTML, and where to go online to learn more about developing your own custom Tumblr themes.

Exploring Tumblr's Theme Garden

Of the roughly 46 million people currently on Tumblr, over 3 million of them are still using the default Redux by Jacob theme, shown in Figure 9-1. While that statistic might have something to do with the number of stagnant Tumblr accounts that were started and then abandoned, the prevalence of the Redux theme might have a whole lot more to do with people's fear of "messing up" their blog or breaking something in its workings that they won't know how to fix.

Figure 9-1: The default Redux by Jacob is Tumblr's most popular theme.

In truth, however, searching through themes — and changing yours often until you find the one that's just perfect — is part of the fun of having a Tumblr blog.

Searching for themes

To get started searching for themes, point your browser to Tumblr's Theme Garden at www.tumblr.com/themes/, shown in Figure 9-2. You may also access this page by clicking the Themes link in the footer of most of your non-Dashboard pages.

Figure 9-2: Search through free and premium themes in Tumblr's Theme Garden.

At the top of the page, you'll see a cartoony hill-and-sky scene with links you can click to learn more about theme development and submit a custom theme to the Garden. There's also a cute population sign that shows how many themes are currently in the Garden.

At the foot of the rolling green hills are four navigation tabs, and underneath that is a listing of all the themes. Each theme, as illustrated in Figure 9-3, includes the theme's name, author, thumbnail image, and number of people using the theme, along with buttons to preview and install it.

Figure 9-3: Each theme listed includes the name, author, thumbnail, Preview button, and Install button.

To change the sorting order of themes listed on this page, click one of these navigation tabs:

- ✔ **Featured:** Themes that the folks at Tumblr deem to be "feature-worthy" are showcased here and are identified by a red Featured banner that sits diagonally across their top-left corners. You'll also see these themes listed in the Themes area of the Customize Theme page.

- ✔ **Premium:** These themes, which have blue Premium banners on their top-left corners, are custom-designed with all kinds of specialized features and customizable appearance options. Expect to shell out anywhere from $9–$49 for these beauties. Some themes even include integration with other third-party add-ons from sources such as SoundCloud, iTunes, Bandcamp, Songkick, Flickr, Instagram, Big Cartel, and Typekit. The MARS Theme (`http://mars.stylehatch.co/`) is a great example of how robust a Premium theme can be.

- ✔ **Recent:** This page displays a seemingly endless list of themes added recently to the Theme Garden, including regular, Featured, and Premium. Theme listings here include the number of people currently using each theme.

- ✔ **Popular:** Sorting by Popular will display a list of Featured, Premium, and regular themes according to the number of people using each one, from most to least.

Previewing themes

When you see a theme in the Theme Garden that looks interesting to you, you can preview it by clicking the gray Preview button at the bottom of the theme box to launch the theme in a new browser tab or window. Feel free to cruise around to see how the theme looks and functions. Most preview pages include examples of each kind of post (photo, text, video, and such), so you have a clear idea of how the theme looks, and where on the page visitors can view such features as notes, comments, and tags.

Installing themes

Installing a Tumblr theme from the Theme Garden is fast and easy:

1. **From the Theme Garden listing, click the thumbnail or the Install button of the theme you'd like to install.**

   The theme's installation page opens in your browser, looking similar to Figure 9-4.

Figure 9-4: The Theme Install page will have a place to select your blog and install the theme.

2. **On the right side of the page, select the name of your blog from the Choose Blog drop-down menu.**

   If you have more than one blog, the primary blog will be listed first in the menu, with any secondary blogs listed below it.

3. **From here, you may install or purchase the theme:**

   • *Install:* Click the Install Theme button and your new theme will be installed immediately.

   • *Purchase:* Click the Purchase Theme button, and a small pop-up window will appear where you can input your credit card number and other information. Click the Next button to proceed to checkout or click the PayPal link to purchase credits for your Tumblr account (which you may then use to purchase and install themes). After your credit card or payment has been approved, you can proceed with the installation by clicking the Install button.

After you've installed your new theme, you may want to customize some of the theme's settings. Check out Chapter 1 for more about customizing your free or Premium theme.

Editing a Theme's HTML

Editing the HTML on a Tumblr theme is a bit tricky for the average user, so unless you think you have a pretty good handle on HTML and CSS, you might want to leave the HTML theme-editing to the pros. On the other hand, if you do know some HTML and CSS or if you're feeling adventurous and think you can figure it out as you go, then by all means, jump in! If you try, you might very well succeed.

Examining your theme's code

To begin editing your theme, click the Edit HTML button at the top of your blog's Customize Theme page. You can access the Customize Theme page by clicking the Customize Theme button on your Dashboard sidebar. Clicking this button opens the HTML panel for your selected theme, as shown in Figure 9-5.

If you examine the code in the HTML Editing panel on the left side of your screen by scrolling up and down, you'll see that the code is broken up into logical sections, like a regular HTML webpage:

- **Meta tags:** At the top, there are Meta tags that control some of the customizable features of the theme.

- **CSS:** Below the Meta tags, you'll find a section of custom CSS used to style and position the content within the theme.

✔ **JavaScript:** You may also see some JavaScript code for adding IDs for Google analytics and linking to external jQuery and JavaScript files.

✔ **HTML:** Beneath the JavaScript code, you'll see the HTML, which blocks out the different types of posts you can create on your Tumblr blog using variables and {block} tags.

HTML   Preview

Figure 9-5: Click the Edit HTML button on the Customize page to open the HTML Editing panel on the left with a preview area on the right.

Tumblr uses two kinds of tags in its page code: variables and blocks. The *variables* let you insert dynamic content into your theme, similar to how WordPress works, if you're familiar with that. For example, you can create a link to a post by adding the {Permalink} tag to an anchor link, like this:

```
<h1><a href="{Permalink}">{Title}</a></h1>
```

By contrast, *block tags* are used to build the different sections of the HTML page for different post types (such as Photo or Text). For instance, you might use the {block:Link} tags to build an area on your theme for that type of post:

```
{block:Link}
<h2 class="the-link"><a href="{URL}"
        {Target}>{Name}</a></h2>
{block:Description}{Description}
          {/block:Description}
{/block:Link}
```

Keep in mind that for your theme to function properly, it must include blocks for all seven post types, plus photosets and answers: `Text`, `Photo`, `Photoset`, `Quote`, `Link`, `Chat`, `Audio`, `Video`, and `Answer`. For an example of how this might look, refer to the HTML in the default Redux Tumblr theme.

Locating an element's class or ID

To customize the look of a particular element, first you need to determine the CSS selector (tag, class, or ID) for the element you want to change. After you identify the CSS selector, you can locate it in the CSS section of your theme's code, and add to, delete, or edit that selector's style declarations.

To help you find any particular CSS selector in your theme, look no further than your own browser. Most browsers offer free CSS inspection tools and plug-ins. While they all work in the same general way, each has its own user interface and functionality. Be sure to consult your particular browser's help files for assistance.

Here is some general information about the most popular browser CSS inspection tools:

✔ **Firefox:** Download and install the Firebug or InspectThis Add-on to your copy of Firefox. After the add-on is installed, right-click the element you want to change and then select Inspect Element.

You can download Firebug at `http://getfirebug.com/html` or get a copy of InspectThis from `https://addons.mozilla.org/en-US/firefox/addon/inspectthis/`.

✔ **Chrome:** Right-click anywhere in your browser window and select the Inspect Element option from the context menu. This opens the Inspect Elements panel at the bottom of your browser window. You may then hover your cursor over the HTML in the code area of the Inspect Element panel to identify the class or ID of an element in the preview pane above. Figure 9-6 shows an example of what that might look like.

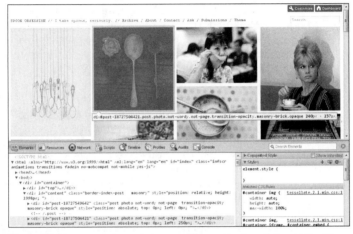

Figure 9-6: Use your browser's Inspect Element feature to locate the ID or class of an element within an existing Tumblr theme.

✔ **Safari:** Select Preferences from the General Safari Settings menu at the far-right side of your browser. When the dialog box opens, select the Advanced tab and put a check mark in the box that says Show Develop Menu in Menu Bar, and then close the window by clicking its X. You may then right-click anywhere on your page and choose Inspect Element from the context menu to open the Inspect Element panel in your browser window. This tool works very similarly to Firebug for Firefox.

✔ **Opera:** Opera has recently integrated the Dragonfly inspection tool into its suite of developer tools. To access Dragonfly, right-click anywhere in your browser window, choose the Inspect Element option from the context menu; then click the element you want to change. You can then view that element's properties in the Inspection panel at the bottom of your browser window. To learn more about how Dragonfly works, visit www.opera.com/dragonfly/.

✔ **Internet Explorer:** Download and install a copy of the free Internet Explorer Developer Toolbar from www.microsoft.com/download/en/details. aspx?id=18359. Once installed, choose Tools⇨ Developer Tools to open the Developer Toolbar at the bottom of your screen. You may then choose an icon on the toolbar and click the element on the page that you'd like to learn more about.

Editing an element's class or ID

All of these browsers' Inspect Element features work essentially the same in that you use the tools to identify the class or ID of a particular element. After you've identified the ID or class, you may then go into the HTML and CSS code of your theme and modify that element's properties.

For example, if you want to make the background color of the Heading 1 <h1> element red with the text color set to white in the Georgia font, locate the style for <h1> in the CSS area of your theme's code and edit the style to something like this:

```
h1 {background-color: #D33; color: #FFF;
font-family: Georgia, "Times New Roman",
Times, serif;}
```

Some themes are far more complex than others, utilizing an external CSS (Cascading Style Sheets) file. In those cases, you can find the link to that external file, follow it to its source, and identify the property. You may then create a new external CSS file and add a link to it in your theme, or simply update the property in the Add Custom CSS box in the Advanced editing area of the Customize Theme panel.

Exploring the Basics of Creating a Theme

The previous section of this chapter lays out some basic skills for editing a theme's HTML by examining the code, locating an element's class or ID, and then editing the styles in the HTML and CSS. It also covers adding custom CSS to override your theme's CSS (in the Appearance section at the bottom of the Customize Appearance page). If any of those skills seem difficult or confusing to you, you might want to postpone creating your own Tumblr theme until you've had a bit of practice with HTML and CSS. In addition, if you plan to develop complex Tumblr themes, you might also want to take a look at some tutorials in JavaScript, jQuery, and PHP.

 You can find all kinds of wonderful free tutorials about HTML and CSS online. Two of my personal favorite sites are www. w3schools.com and http://reference.sitepoint. com/html. You may also want to check out *HTML, XHTML & CSS For Dummies,* 7th Edition, by Ed Tittel and Jeff Noble.

Keep in mind that the more you know, the better you'll be able to design and develop your own Tumblr themes — or at least get familiar with the structure of existing themes in Tumblr's Theme Garden.

Gathering the tools you need

Before you develop or build your theme, you need to come up with a design for it. That involves design skills and working knowledge of one or more drawing, web-graphic, and photo-editing software programs. The most popular programs include Adobe Illustrator, Fireworks, and Photoshop, but you could also use any of the free, open-source software alternatives such as GIMP, DrawPlus, Inkscape, Photoscape, or Picasa.

After you've designed your new theme, you need to optimize all your web graphics and build your theme as a standard HTML/CSS web page. For best results, you may want to consider using web-development software such as Dreamweaver or Coda. With a WYSIWYG (what you see is what you get) or coding program, you'll be able to develop your theme even faster than you would by using a simple text editor like Notepad or TextEdit.

Following a theme-creation workflow

Everyone has his or her own way of working, but if you're new to Tumblr theme design, you might be open to suggestions about best practices and workflows that can maximize your effectiveness and make you as productive as possible.

Here's an example of one Tumblr theme-creation workflow that you might adopt for your own projects:

1. Design your theme in Photoshop or another software program.

2. Optimize all your web graphics as JPG, GIF, or PNG files.

3. Build your theme as a standard web page with HTML/ CSS and JavaScript as needed using a web or code editor such as Dreamweaver or CODA.

4. Convert your HTML into Tumblr-friendly markup using *variables* and *blocks,* as defined earlier in this chapter. For example, instead of writing

   ```
   <title>Our first theme</title>
   ```

   you'd convert your code to

   ```
   <title>{Title}</title>
   ```

   The actual title text will be input through the Customize Themes panel. For a complete listing of Tumblr's markup parameters, see www.tumblr.com/ docs/en/custom_themes.

5. Upload any supporting files such as images, CSS, and JavaScript files to Tumblr.

To upload your files to Tumblr's server, go to www. tumblr.com/themes/upload_static_file, as shown in Figure 9-7, where you can select and upload the individual files for your theme.

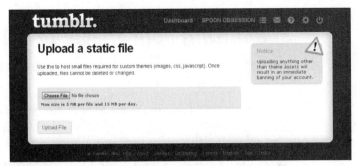

Figure 9-7: Use Tumblr's Upload page to upload your theme's supporting files.

You then need to edit the paths to these resources in your theme's code. For example, say that you have an image with a link like this:

```
<img src="images/datebg.png">
```

After uploading the image to Tumblr, your new link source may look more like this:

```
<img src="http://static.tumblr.com/
s7blpfm/pa1evxo8q/datebg.png">
```

Uploaded files can be a maximum of 5MB each, and you can upload up to 15MB of files per day.

Keep in mind that uploaded files cannot be deleted or changed, so upload with care.

6. Test your theme on your own Tumblr account and fix any errors you encounter.

7. Submit your completed theme to Tumblr through the Theme Garden. For information about this process, refer to the next section in this chapter.

By the time you're finished with your first Tumblr theme, you'll have had a lot more practice designing and building themes than you might have expected. Any new themes you create after that should go much more smoothly and take a lot less time.

Submitting your theme to Tumblr

When you're ready to upload your custom theme to Tumblr's Theme Garden, follow these steps:

1. **Open the Tumblr Theme Submission page** at www.tumblr.com/themes/new, **shown in Figure 9-8.**

Figure 9-8: Be sure to read Tumblr's Submission Requirements before uploading your custom theme.

You'll also find a Submit a Theme link that points to this page in the upper-right corner of the Tumblr Theme Garden at www.tumblr.com/themes/.

2. **Before you do anything else, read the Requirements listing in the sidebar on the right side of the page.**

Tumblr encourages users to create and submit new themes to the Theme Garden. Before you do that, however, make absolutely sure that you carefully follow all the submission rules. If you don't, your account may be permanently banned, which (obviously) you don't want to happen.

Your theme can have no external assets such as images or css files (they must be hosted on Tumblr's site using their file uploader), all third-party widgets must be options, and the theme must support all post types and standard tags. In addition, the whole enchilada has to take up no more space than 64 KB — and above all, the theme must "meet the aesthetic standards of Tumblr."

3. **If you're 100% positive you've met the Submission Requirements, enter a title for your theme in the Title field.**

Your title can be anything you like, such as "Superduper" or "Sue's Amazing Theme" but if you can, try to name it something short, cool, and memorable like "Stars & Night."

4. **Paste your HTML code into the Source Code text box.**

5. **In the Screenshot area, click the Choose File button to browse for and select a screenshot graphic of your theme.**

The graphic can be JPG or PNG at 72 ppi, and should be exactly 375 x 250 pixels.

6. **Check the box that says that you certify you're the theme's author.**

Read this document, too, to make sure you agree with the terms.

7. **Click the Submit Theme for Approval button.**

Now you sit back, relax, and wait for an e-mail from Tumblr to find out whether they've accepted your theme into the Theme Garden.

Most themes submitted this way will either not be accepted or will be added to the Recent Themes listing in the Theme Garden.

If you want your theme to be listed among the Premium Themes, however, keep in mind that it might not happen; Tumblr's standards are very high. Even so, if you're confident and want to see whether your theme meets their standards, you can e-mail Tumblr at support@tumblr.com to let them know you're "interested in participating in their beta program as a Premium Theme designer."

Exploring Online Tumblr Theme Tutorials

Learning all the ins and outs of Tumblr theme development can be a real challenge; there are currently no comprehensive tutorials or training programs available. What you will find, however, is a mishmash of instructions and videos that each provide a small piece in the puzzle of how it all works!

One decent (if slightly dated) tutorial is Creating a Tumblr Theme by Jose Argudo Blanco (http://joseargudo.com) on the PACKT Publishing site at www.packtpub.com/article/creating-a-tumblr-theme. There you'll find step-by-step instructions on how to convert the tags and other markup in your HTML/CSS page into a ready-to-use Tumblr theme.

For a free Tumblr framework to get your Tumblr themes started faster than you would probably do by hand-coding from scratch, download Galen Gidman's (http://galengidman.com/) framework files at https://github.com/galengidman/tumblr-framework.

For additional tutorials and videos about building your own custom Tumblr Themes, check out the following pages:

- PSD to HTML tuts: `http://psdtohtmltuts.com/8-useful-articles-to-jump-into-the-basics-of-html-to-tumblr-themes/`

- Build Internet: `http://buildinternet.com/2010/04/things-to-know-about-custom-tumblr-theme-design/`

- Nettuts+: `http://net.tutsplus.com/tutorials/html-css-techniques/new-plus-tutorial-tumblr-theme-design-start-to-finish/`

- Lynda.com: `www.lynda.com/Twitter-tutorials/Up-and-Running-with-Tumblr/95698-2.html`

Chapter 10

Ten Useful Third-Party Apps for Tumblr

*T*hird-party applications, or *apps,* are special programs written by a person or team of individuals outside a particular company to work with specific operating systems or software developed by that company.

In terms of Tumblr, a third-party developer would be any person or party outside of Tumblr developing an app specifically for Tumblr's open-source *application programming interface* (API). Apps typically enhance existing software in some way by adding new features or integrating the existing service with another service, such as linking Tumblr to Facebook and Twitter. Apps come in several forms such as plug-ins, add-ons, extensions, standalone programs, or even hacks that you use to modify existing features and performance.

New apps for Tumblr are being developed nearly every day for all kinds of uses. Some of them are wonderful and grow in popularity quickly, while others never catch on or simply disappear too soon due to lack of funding. In this chapter, I've pulled together a list of the ten best third-party apps currently available for Tumblr. I hope you enjoy them!

HelloTxt

There's no denying that social media accounts are hot right now. Chances are you currently have at least one other social media account besides your Tumblr blog. In fact, most people will already have accounts with Facebook and Twitter before signing up for Tumblr, and then quickly branch out to more social media sites like Pinterest, LinkedIn, Dribble, Google Plus, WordPress, Flickr, Instagram, Last.fm, and a handful of others.

With all those accounts, one of the big questions on every-one's minds is, "How can I manage all my posts across all my accounts so that if I update one, the rest will update automatically?" The answer: HelloTxt.

HelloTxt is one of several new status-manager services; it helps you update your status across all your social networks and microblogs from the privacy of your own computer, tablet, e-mail, or mobile phone (see Figure 10-1). To sign up, visit www. hellotxt.com and follow the onscreen instructions to create your account and start synchronizing your posts.

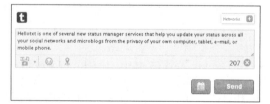

Figure 10-1: Get HelloTxt to help manage your status across all your popular social media accounts.

Ping.fm

Ping.fm is another social media updating service you might be interested in using to integrate with your Tumblr account.

With a Ping.fm account, you can post from your browser, iPhone, and iPod touch, do WPA and SMS text messaging, blast out messages from your e-mail account or instant messaging service, and connect to over 100 web and desktop apps from other third-party developers. (See Figure 10-2.)

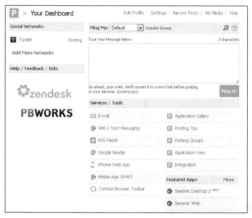

Figure 10-2: Use Ping.fm to "post from anywhere to anywhere," including to Tumblr and your other preferred social media sites.

To create your free Ping.fm account, visit `www.ping.fm`, where you enter your e-mail address and desired password.

After your account is setup, you can add your social media accounts to your Ping.fm network and start a-postin'. For a walkthrough on Ping.fm's services, see `http://web.appstorm.net/how-to/microblogging/update-social-networks-with-ping-fm/`.

Blip.fm

If you love music and love being online, but you don't want to have to pay to listen to your favorite songs, enter Blip.fm, the social Internet radio station that lets you listen to any song for free. What's more, with Blip.fm you'll have access to millions (yes, millions!) of songs to create your own free Internet radio station or listen to the stations created by others. You can even become a DJ of sorts to share your radio casts of streaming MP3s with your friends on your favorite social media sites including Facebook, Twitter, and Tumblr.

Before you can share your free DJ station with your Tumblr followers, you need to create a Blip.fm account by visiting www.blip.fm.

The welcome page, shown in Figure 10-3, asks for your DJ name and e-mail address to sign up for an account. Then, after you're registered, you can cruise around the site to find the music you're interested in hearing. You can then generate as many music "blips" as you like to share on Tumblr.

Figure 10-3: With Blip.fm, you can create "blips" of songs from your own free streaming Internet radio station to share on Tumblr.

TumblrStats

If you've ever wondered if there's a place you can go to learn more about your Tumblr blog's stats, there's an app for that. Go to www.tumblrstats.com in your favorite browser and type in the name of your blog in the What Is Your Tumblr Username? field. To view your site's stats, press Enter/Return and give the server a few seconds to process your data.

The browser should generate some basic stats to read while it finishes crunching your data. When the job is complete, as shown in Figure 10-4, you'll see facts about your blog from basic information like start date, title and description, to more interesting complex data including your total number of posts, average number of posts per day, percentage of post types, and posting frequency.

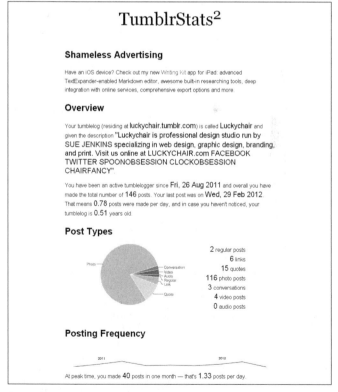

Figure 10-4: Check your Tumblr blog stats at Tumblrstats.com.

Zemanta

If you like freebies, you'll love Zemanta, a free tool that helps you enrich your social media posts with relevant pictures, links, articles, and tags, which can help make them more popular and sticky, garnering you more followers in your quest to take over the Internet.

Zemanta, shown in Figure 10-5, can be installed on your end as a browser extension or bookmarklet for Firefox, Internet Explorer, Chrome, and Safari. It can also be added as a server-side plug-in for WordPress, MovableType, Drupal, and Joomla!

Zemanta

Figure 10-5: Get Zemanta as a browser extension to help promote your content with relevant images, articles, links, and more.

To find out how easy it is to use, visit www.zemanta.com and check out the free demo. There you'll see dynamic intelligence at work, as the demo shows you how to promote your content by adding images, related articles, in-text links, and tags relevant to your post. Hubba hubba.

Missing e

If you're ready to rev up your Tumblr account, definitely check out Missing e, the free browser extension that boosts your ability to navigate, post, and socialize on Tumblr (see Figure 10-6). You can download and install Missing e on your Firefox, Safari, or Chrome browser at http://missing-e.com.

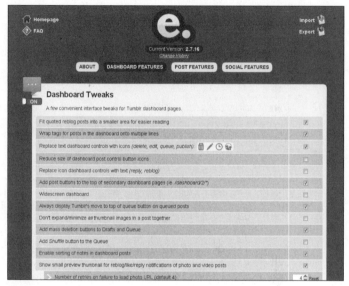

Figure 10-6: Missing e is a useful browser extension for Tumblr.

At this time, there are currently 15 interface changes, tools, and special features included in the software to enhance your Tumblr posts, including a magnifier, timestamps, reblog enhancements, mass editor tweaks, and more.

LinkWithin Related Posts

The LinkWithin Related Posts widget is an SEO-smart blog add-on that lets you display and suggest related posts at the bottom of each post, as shown in Figure 10-7, in an "elegant and unobtrusive" way. Agreed!

Figure 10-7: Add the LinkWithin Related Posts widget to your Tumblr to help keep visitors engaged with other posts on your site.

Studies show that the longer visitors stay on a site, the more likely they are to want your products or services, or if you don't have any of those to offer, at the very least, related posts can help you keep your new and regular visitors happy.

To use this widget, visit the LinkWithin website at www.link within.com and follow the instructions to enter your e-mail address, blog URL, platform, and number of stories. You are then taken to a page with some code that you can paste into your site. This widget must be installed by hand, which means you'll need to edit your theme's HTML with some free code. If you follow the directions, the process should be quick and painless.

Tumblr Tag Clouds

A *tag cloud* is a list of hyperlinked tags or keywords on a website that helps visitors to visualize the importance of each word by its relative size and color within the list. The bigger the word, the more important it is on a site, whereas the smaller the word, the less important it is compared to the rest.

Sometimes tag clouds are alphabetized but more often the words are floating in a blob or confined area without any seeming order to their placement within the cloud. Regardless of how they're organized, the links, when clicked, take visitors to another location within the site that features content related to each word.

You can add a free, customizable tag-cloud generator to your Tumblr blog by pasting some code into your site at the location where you'd like it to appear. To grab a copy of the free code for your Tumblr blog, or to preview what the tag cloud for your Tumblr blog might look like, visit Heather Rivers' website at `http://rive.rs/projects/tumblr-tag-clouds`, and follow the instructions on the page. (See Figure 10-8.)

Figure 10-8: Preview the tag cloud for your Tumblr blog before adding the code to your site.

Pikchur

If you're one of the millions of people obsessed with taking photos with your camera phone, you're going to love this app. Pikchur is an online service that lets you upload your photos and videos in one place and share them automatically with all your linked social media and micro-blogging sites.

Pikchur works with Tumblr, Twitter, Facebook, Flickr, FriendFeed, and Plurk, just to name a few. It's also mobile-friendly and offers a pro account service with access to traffic stats on your picture posts.

To sign up for your Pikchur account, visit `http://pikchur.com`. You can sign in with either Twitter or Facebook, or enter an e-mail address, display name, and password.

Once you're logged in, you can link to your social media accounts, start posting your photos, view your recent activity, upload images (as shown in Figure 10-9), and search for other Pikchur users to follow.

Figure 10-9: Simplify your picture posting with Pikchur.

Postling

Of the ten third-party applications recommended in this chapter, Postling is by far the most popular tool used by professionals and businesses. That's because it combines social media management with alerts and insights and allows for multiple users so everyone within an organization can have a hand in keeping your social media accounts humming with activity.

With Postling, you can unify and streamline your publishing, put your posts on a schedule, and review and respond to your comments in one location. It even has a magical Suggestion Engine that can recommend when to make special connections with new influential followers, and can track Yelp and CitySearch reviews so that any time there's a new post about your service, you can read about it in real time.

Postling has been recently featured in *The New York Times,* TechCrunch, *The Wall Street Journal,* and Mashable. The only possible barrier between you and this incredible service is the thickness of your wallet. Posting costs $1 for the first 30 days of service, but after that, the fee is $3 per month per social media account. So, for instance, if you have one Twitter account, two Facebook accounts, and one Tumblr blog, that will cost you a cool $12 per month.

To find out whether Postling is right for you, take the tour at `http://postling.com/tour_home.php` (see Figure 10-10). If it is a good fit, you can sign up for an account at `https://postling.com/`.

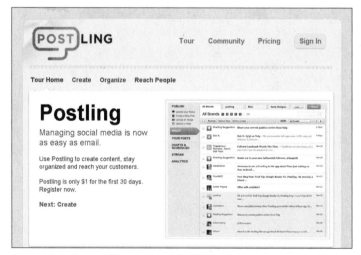

Figure 10-10: Get Postling, the smart businesses' social media-management tool.

Appendix

Tumblr Resources

• •

In This Appendix

▶ Using Tumblr's Help Center

▶ Finding Tumblr help online

• •

The best social media sites keep their users happy by offering easy-to-use, easy-to-access help files. On Tumblr, as long as you have Internet access, you can search through the Help Center 24/7. Just click the Help (?) button on the Dashboard menu, enter your question or search term, and click the magnifying-glass icon.

In addition to searching through the Help Center on Tumblr. com, you can find all kinds of tutorials, tips, tricks, hacks, social media tools, extensions, add-ons, and training videos online to help you navigate your way through the wonderful world of Tumblr, both as a user and as a theme developer.

This appendix shows you how to get the most out of using Tumblr's Help Center — and provides recommendations for the best online tutorials and videos about using Tumblr. There's even a short section at the end about where to go for help if you want to become a developer for Tumblr extensions and third-party apps.

Using the Help Center

Whenever you have a question about how Tumblr works, or if you simply want to find out more about a particular feature, find stats on Tumblr's users and development team, or see whether anyone's encountered a bug you've run across, head to Tumblr's Help Center at www.tumblr.com/help.

The Help Center page, shown in Figure A-1, has a search field at the top for you to enter your search term and a blue magnifying-glass button you can click to submit your query. Below the search-field area, you'll see a listing of the most frequently asked questions and short answers to them.

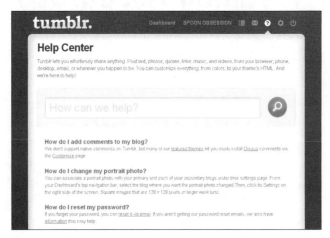

Figure A-1: The Tumblr Help Center is available 24/7 to anyone with an Internet connection.

When you search for a particular term, the search results will appear below the search field. Then you may click any links within the search results to drill deeper into the answer to your inquiry. For example, if you want to know how to reset your password, the answer is `If you forget your password, you can reset it via e-mail`. Embedded within that sentence is a link to the Forgot Password page, which provides further details about how this process works.

Finding Tumblr Help Online

As comprehensive as the Tumblr Help Center is, you may occasionally find that there is no precise answer to your question. When that happens, you'll likely see a "sorry we can't find that" message such as

Sorry, we can't find that.

Please email us and we'll help you out right away.

When a Tumblr Help search is unsuccessful, you have three options:

  ✓ **Try searching for different search terms until you find an acceptable answer.** Sometimes finding the right answer is a matter of just the right phrasing or using the right combination of keywords in your search.

  ✓ **Send the folks at Tumblr an e-mail requesting the answer to your question.** You can reach them at support@tumblr.com. You'll even find a link for this e-mail embedded in the "sorry we can't find that" message in the Help Center. In most cases, you'll get a reply from Tumblr within 24 hours.

  ✓ **Google it, baby!** Or use another preferred search engine to search for the answer to your question or inquiry. Search engines provide you with a results listing of possible answers. There's no guarantee you'll find the answer there either, but Google's database is much, much bigger, so you're more likely to find something useful.

When you're searching for help online, you may discover that some sites tend to have better answers than others. Because Tumblr is a website tool of sorts, you're likeliest to find the best answers, most comprehensive information, and helpful tutorials about web design and Tumblr on websites that cater to web designers. Two examples are www.smashingmagazine.com and www.webdesignerdepot.com.

Even so, finding the right answers can be an exhausting and time-consuming task. To save you time and potential headaches, the following sections were created with you in mind. You'll find three lists of links offering some of the best information about using Tumblr, designing for Tumblr, and creating custom Tumblr themes.

Using Tumblr, tricks, and hacks

If you've read everything in the book from the start up to this point, you should have a handle on everything you need to know about how to use Tumblr. Nonetheless, some questions may linger — and studies show that hearing an answer more than once from a different source can help reinforce new knowledge. The following lists of links will help you with general Tumblr usage information, as well as provide you with tips, tricks, tutorials, and other goodies to enhance your Tumblr experience:

- **Huffington Post:** "Tumblr Guide 101"

  ```
  www.huffingtonpost.com/2011/05/06/
  tumblr-guide-tips-and-tricks_n_858724.
  html#s275319&title=Basics_The_Dashboard
  ```

- **Webmonkey:** "Getting Started with Tumblr"

  ```
  www.webmonkey.com/2010/02/get_started_
  with_tumblr/
  ```

- **Tumblring:** "Tips, Tricks, and All Things Tumblr"

  ```
  http://tumblring.net/
  ```

- **How to Use Tumblr:** "Tips, Tricks, Tutorials, and Goodies"

  ```
  http://howtousetumblr.com/
  ```

- **I Love Tumblr:** "Tips for Bloggers Who Love Tumblr"

  ```
  www.ilovetumblr.com/
  ```

- **Tumblr:** "Tips from Tumblr Users"

  ```
  www.tumblr.com/tagged/tumblr-tips
  ```

- **Tutorials & More:** Tutorials, backgrounds, animated gifs, favicons, music players, and more

  ```
  http://tutorialsandmore.tumblr.com/
  ```

- **FreeCodeSource.com:** Tumblr codes, effects, tutorials, and other freebies

  ```
  http://freecodesource.com/tumblr-codes/
  index
  ```

- **Cherrybam.com:** Themes, backgrounds, layouts, tutorials, and tips

  ```
  www.cherrybam.com/tumblr-tutorials.php
  ```

Designing for Tumblr

Although designing for Tumblr is a bit different from designing for a regular website, it is similar to designing for other blog platforms such as WordPress. The following links should help you with the design side of creating your Tumblr blog:

- ✔ **Inspired Magazine:** "7 Ways to Design a Useful & Customizable Tumblr Theme"

    http://inspiredm.com/designing-tumblr-themes/

- ✔ **Smashing Magazine:** Tutorials on web design, coding, graphics, and UX design

    www.smashingmagazine.com/tag/web-design/

- ✔ **Webdesigner Depot:** Step-by-step tutorial on designing for Tumblr

    www.webdesignerdepot.com/2011/05/design-a-forest-inspired-tumblr-theme-in-photoshop/

- ✔ **Net Magazine:** "The Web Designer's Guide to Tumblr"

    www.netmagazine.com/features/web-designers-guide-tumblr

- ✔ **Net.tutsplus.com:** "Tumblr Theme Design – Start to Finish" ($19/month for unlimited site access)

    http://net.tutsplus.com/tutorials/html-css-techniques/new-plus-tutorial-tumblr-theme-design-start-to-finish/

- ✔ ***Theme Tumblr Like a Pro*** ($29 e-book)

    http://rockablepress.com/books/theme-tumblr-like-a-pro/

Building Tumblr themes

As mentioned in Chapter 9, building your own Tumblr themes presupposes some knowledge of HTML and CSS, and possibly some familiarity with JavaScript, jQuery, and PHP. If you have a general knowledge of web design, and think you have what it takes to design your own Tumblr themes (or tweak an existing one), you should find the following links about building Tumblr themes quite useful:

- ✔ **WikiHow:** "Tumblr Theme Creation"

    www.wikihow.com/Create-a-Custom-Page-on-Tumblr

- ✔ **Your Blog Sources:** Cute graphic freebies, interesting code hacks, and answers to your theme questions

    `http://yourblogsources.tumblr.com/`

- ✔ **TutBox:** "How to Make Your Own Two-Column Tumblr Theme"

    `http://tutbox.tumblr.com/tumblr-theme-tutorial-how-to-make-your-own-two-column`

- ✔ **Monique Tendencia:** "Updated Theme Tutorial"

    `http://tutorials.moniquetendencia.com/new-theme-tutorial`

- ✔ **eHow:** "How to Make a Custom HTML for Tumblr"

    `www.ehow.com/how_8637332_make-custom-html-tumblr.html`

- ✔ **Line 25:** Getting started with custom theme design

    `http://line25.com/articles/getting-started-with-tumblr-and-custom-theme-design`

- ✔ **Spyre Studios:** "30 Awesome Examples of Custom Tumblr Designs"

    `http://spyrestudios.com/30-awesome-custom-tumblr-blog-designs/`

- ✔ **Packt:** "Creating a Tumblr Theme"

    `www.packtpub.com/article/creating-a-tumblr-theme`

- ✔ **Design Shack:** "Introduction to Developing a Custom Tumblr Blog Theme"

    `http://designshack.net/articles/html/introduction-to-developing-a-custom-tumblr-blog-theme/`

- ✔ **1stwebdesigner:** "How to Create a Tumblr Theme (Code Structure)"

    `www.1stwebdesigner.com/tutorials/how-to-create-tumblr-theme/`

If you're looking for ways to extend or enhance your Tumblr blog, be sure to check out the ten useful third-party apps for Tumblr discussed in Chapter 10.

Index